The **Gratitude Book Project**®

Best of Pets

The Gratitude Book Project® Team
A Division of Kozik Rocha, Inc.

Want to be a published author?

Book writing, publishing, and consulting services provided by Kozik Rocha, Inc.

Write Your Book

Write a Book in a Weekend® is an online, virtual course that guides you in writing a "short and powerful" book in two days with pre-formatted templates, how-to information, and expert guidance. Find out more and and get a FREE "Book Writing Planner" at WriteWithDonna.com.

Publish Your Book

"Done for You" Publishing Services offers everything from editing and proofreading to interior formatting and cover design, while providing personal connection and top-rate customer service. Find out more at DoneForYouPublishing.com.

Get Answers to Your Book Writing and Publishing Questions

If you're struggling with what to write about or organizing your material, or if you're frustrated because you can't find answers about how the book publishing process works, get a "Big Breakthrough Session" with two-time award-winning author and publishing expert Donna Kozik. More at MyBigBreakthroughSession.com.

Not sure what you need?

E-mail business manager Dina Rocha with your questions at Dina@MyBigBusinessCard.com or call us anytime at 619-923-3082 to talk about it.

Contents

Acknowledgments

The Gratitude Book Project: Best of Pets touches on one of the few subjects that level the playing field between cultures, economic status, and religious and political differences. Our pets do not care what belief system we subscribe to, how famous we are, or how much prestige or power we do or don't have. They do not judge us and they are quick to forgive us our shortcomings. They have been known to bring out the best in people and many of us strive to live up to the high regard our pets hold us in.

Though this book is about the cherished critters in our lives, it took a bit of human effort to get it into your hands. To keep gratitude in motion we must express our thanks whenever possible.

So a big shout out to the following for being a part of bringing the *Best of Pets* to life is in order:

Donna Kozik, *Editor who shares her space with The Gratitude Book Project Mascots, Foggy and Felina*
These cats rule the roost around here, do a great job of holding down the offices when we're away, and are a constant source of work place entertainment. Warning: Be cautious when entering the offices of Kozik Rocha, Inc. as Foggy is often perched on top of the door making sure everyone is working.

Dina Rocha, *Publication Manager and Keeper of Canine Comrades, Angel, Sammy, and Jordan*
These critters are the loves of Dina's life and help her to greet every day with tail-wagging positivity. With their help, Dina keeps the whole team on the right track.

Michelle Dimsey, *Associate Editor who shares her space with Krash, Boxer Extraordinaire*
This delightful dog has trouble keeping traction on the wood floors, but not on anyone's heart. He has mastered the art of fresh fruit delivery and is the only dog we know who reads—which is, of course, pleasing to a writer.

Deanna McAdams, *Submission Coordinator who lovingly remembers Louie*
This adorable white kitty with black patches on his head was Deanna's first pet and provided her with much love and entertainment. Deanna not only coordinates submissions, she also helps to keep the whole team in the loop.

Becky Cohen, *Cover Designer and Graphic Illustrator, Friend of Weezie, The Frisbee-Playing Black Lab*
Weezie enjoys Frisbee on the beach and is said to swim like an otter. She is a lover of people and has adopted Becky as her own supplemental human even though her family lives across the street. Becky is a true artist whose graphics and illustrations have helped bring pizzazz to this project.

Jodi Brandon, *Proofreader and Provider to JoePa, The Welcome Shepherd*
Perfect timing and ideal circumstances brought these two together—exactly the combination needed for someone in charge of monitoring the little details most of us miss.

Susan Veach, *Layout Artist and Formatter Protected in Spirit by Fred, the 65-Pound Scaredy Cat*
For ten years Fred, a lab mix, stood guard—under the bed—protecting Susan and her family from all enemies foreign and domestic including frightening leaves, vicious snow and anything else that fell from the sky, allowing Susan to focus her formatting expertise on the project at hand.

Jenni Busboom, *Assistant Proofreader and Cat Lover*
As a child, Jenni's family had 5 cats who all had kittens at the same time—cat heaven for Jenni and her sister! Her most recent cat, Cato, gave her sixteen years of feline entertainment. Jenni does a great job of helping to make the rest of us look good.

Mallory Egger, *Media Relations Specialist and Roomie to Pit Bulls Rocky and Bella, who Think They're Lap Dogs*
These Pits not only think they can share Mallory's lap—they also believe themselves to be human, providing their human countless hours of entertainment. Mallory is our newest edition to the team and comes to us with a "can-do" attitude and a sharp media-mindedness.

And finally, thanks to all the creatures, big and small, who have touched our lives and inspired their people—our co-authors—to join us in our continuing effort to keep the wheels of gratitude in constant motion by participating in The Gratitude Book Project Series®.

This is *The Best of Pets*!

Introduction

Humanity has been observing and learning about their own survival and comfort from animals since the beginning of time. Eventually those associations moved beyond the practical and into the realm of full-blown relationships of reciprocated love and affection. Today, in the United States alone, nearly 40 million households have at least one dog and 38 million have at least one cat. But mankind's love of animals doesn't begin and end in loyal canines or frisky felines. From horses, goats, and pigs, to bunnies, rats, birds, llamas, and beyond, people love their furry, feathered, and even sometimes scaly friends.

In fact, most people think of their pets as members of the family. And why not? They provide their humans countless hours of entertainment, companionship, and unconditional love. It's even more than that, though. Before the first edition of *The Gratitude Book Project: Celebrating 365 Days of Gratitude* ever went to press, our co-authors were chomping at the bit for a book dedicated to the expression of love and appreciation for the animals in their lives. After reading some of their stories it became clear that many people have come to rely on their animal friends for more than just love.

Our pets are reducing stress, lowering blood pressure, stimulating empathy and awareness, encouraging social interactions, fighting depression and loneliness, increasing exercise, fostering trust, improving relationships between humans, protecting loved ones and property, and providing a variety of valuable services. In short, they are capable of enhancing, extending, and in some cases, even saving our lives.

For all that our critter companions may do to improve our health and relationships or help us to feel secure, those benefits are the by-products or bonuses—they are rarely the reasons we choose to share our lives with animals. The camaraderie and unreserved affection they give us just for being who we are cannot be compared.

Yet the kind of joy our animals bring to us is not without risk—in these pages you will read of sorrow and of loss. But in spite of the heartbreak that is often beyond consolation, no one seems willing to trade the joy to avoid the pain. So you will also read of a deep, profound, and abiding gratitude that clearly deserves a book of its own!

After all, our pets seem to bring out the best in us and most of us only hope to one day "be the people our animal companions imagine us to be." If our beloved companions could read, they would be honored to be included in *The Best of Pets!*

~ Michelle Dimsey, Associate Editor

Lessons Learned

Many subscribe to the theory that people would lead happier lives and the world would be a far more civilized place if everyone behaved more like their pets. For all of humanity's intelligence and tool using skills, their ability to complicate even the simplicities of life often borders on comical.

You don't have to be a rocket scientist to see there are many things to be learned not only from animals in the wild but from pets as well. There are numerous practical, ethical, behavioral, and even spiritual lessons to be gained from observing and interacting with creatures big and small.

Having pets can teach children about the basics of personal responsibility, patience, and caring for others. It can also develop their awareness about the importance of exercise, discipline, work ethics, and the benefit of play time—although most grown-ups could use a reminder or two about that!

Adults in general might give consideration to spending some time attempting to mimic the animals in their lives to improve their own overall sense of peace and well-being. Animals, by nature, are without pretense. They don't care what their people look like and spend no time being self-critical. They lead simple lives and set the best example of how to be present or in the moment—they never wake up fretting over yesterday or worrying about tomorrow. They know about the importance of stretching before getting up, never turn down a joyride, and excel at letting go and moving

on. Animals give their affection freely, love unconditionally, and offer no judgments. They are loyal and understand the importance of occasional solitude. In packs, they keep each other in check and never bite when growling alone will solve a problem.

In the following section you will see humans are reaping numerous benefits beyond loyalty and affection from their animal companions. They are observing and learning important life lessons as well.

Huckleberry's Lessons

I watch him in his twilight years, a gentle creature who stays close to me now. His eyesight waning, his hearing fading, he stays close to me. He doesn't always greet me when I get home, but he stays close to me when I am home. So different from when he moved in: his shadow frightened him; he lashed out frequently. We worked hard together meeting every challenge, overcoming the fear of unknown objects or people or dogs. Slowly he learned to let go.

He has a built-in pack of followers: people who visit him, people who want him near—their own version of therapy. As they scratch him, he gently rests a paw on an arm…or a shoulder…and he gently nudges for more. He tests more simply now: *How long can I sleep on the sofa before I'm caught? If I slowly stretch my way off the sofa, will she laugh enough to forget to reprimand me?* It's said I saved him, yet he saved me more. He taught me the power of calm and peacefulness in transforming both his life and mine. Together we greet every day—me, so grateful for his presence in my life, and Huckleberry, so close to me now.

~ Lee Ann Seaman

Lee Ann Seaman *lives in Minneapolis, Minn., and has operated Twin Cities Concierge, a personal concierge service, for over 14 years. Her e-mail address is LAS@TCConcierge.com.*

Let Love In

I am eternally grateful for my "small in stature but large in heart" feline, Princess Pushkins. She has helped me overcome fear, shown me unconditional love, and healed my relationships beyond my wildest dreams. When I moved into my apartment in Hove East Sussex 11 years ago, I was unhappy in singledom. Pushkins turned up at my windowsill ready to love and to be loved. She playfully nudged and nestled, laid Sphinx-like on my sleeping belly, and became my alarm clock. We became buddies, so when I started dating Symon, she checked his suitability instantly with fierce bats of her claws and wild scratches. Symon, a lifelong animal lover, was undeterred by her kitty tests as our relationship blossomed. Three years later, happily married now, something drastic happened to Pushkins: her heart opened, and she became a soft, purring lap cat. We all felt this love. She began to assist me in my healing and therapy practice, too. Witches are said to have familiars, and there she was! Today Princess Pushkins is a grand old lady. She continues to help me run the Gratitude Group and never fails to bring joy, love, and healing to all those she meets.

~ *Ann E. O'keife*

Ann O'keife *is a healer, therapist, rune expert, artist, and writer. She facilitates a monthly gratitude group in Shoreham West Sussex. Learn more at LivingLifeFully.net.*

Merlin's Magical Teachings

Out of the blue my girlfriend announced that I needed to get a dog because my heart needed to open more. I defensively answered that nothing was wrong with my heart. I started pondering this idea and thought it was impossible with my travel schedule and already having three cats. A few months later, my friend found my puppy, and two days later he arrived at my house. Merlin is joy on steroids, and he is the happiest creature I have encountered. He has taught me about unconditional love through the way he greets and treats each person—exactly the same way, with unconditional love and enthusiasm. He makes each person feel special. Merlin's loving consistency has taught me to let go of the little and big things in life, and to keep my heart softer and more loving with people. I feel happier, calmer, and more joyful and loving because of Merlin. I am so fortunate to have him in my life, and I give thanks to him every day for his gentle teachings.

~ Bridget Engel

Bridget Engel, *angel intuitive and personal life coach, teaches people how to utilize their intuition and Divine Guidance to create big results in their lives.*

Endless Love

When we decided to get a puppy for my 8-year-old son, I was terribly afraid of animals. In fact, I would not touch an animal, and no one who knew me would have thought I would own a dog (or any pet). I am a great bird watcher. Soon after King, our Brindle Bullmastiff, was delivered to our front door, he quickly learned the house rules and, when he was ready, attended obedience training. For the first 8 to 10 months, things went fine—meaning I would arrive home from work, look through the mail, and head upstairs. One day I was unable to head up the stairs: King had centered himself on the stairs and would not move. He just sat there, looking past me out the window with his tail wagging. Suddenly my son appeared and said, "King!" He immediately jumped off the stairs. At that moment, I got it. King taught me what it felt like to be ignored and treated like an invisible being. I learned that animals have feelings, and for the next 12 years I experienced deep gratitude for his presence in our family, and his endless love and devotion.

~ *Millie Sunday Jett*

Millie Sunday Jett *is a co-author, speaker, registered nurse, lieutenant colonel (retired), and emotional freedom and healing facilitator. Find her at Facebook.com/Millie.Jett or LinkedIn.com/in/MillieSundayJett2cu.*

Horses: Friends and Teachers

Since childhood, horses have blessed me with friendship, unconditional love, and more of an education than I received in any classroom. This valuable lesson from my horse, Trigger, is just one of many I am grateful for. It was a beautiful spring day, and I wanted to spend some quality time bonding with Trigger. I gathered my grooming tools and headed for the pasture, purposely leaving halter and lead rope behind. While I brushed Trigger, he grazed quietly. All was well and peaceful. That is, until I reached for a bottle of fly spray. To show his displeasure, Trigger promptly departed. Every time I approached him, he turned and walked away. Finally he stopped in a fence corner, his rear facing me. In horse language, this isn't a nice gesture! Intuitively, I remembered that by shifting focus from thinking to feeling, I could communicate with Trigger heart-to-heart. I was amazed at how quickly he responded to this new approach. Within seconds, he spun around and softened his stance. This time he didn't move while I used the spray on him. In that moment, without words, I sent Trigger genuine love and appreciation, and he responded by trusting me.

~ *Leslie Hagerich*

Leslie Hagerich, *CPC, empowers individuals and organizations by getting to the "heart" of what motivates people and performance. You can find her at LeadersEdgeCoaching.com.*

Elvis

Llama Love

Twelve years ago I fell in love at first sight with a lonely looking, 2-year-old llama for sale in a herd of much older males. His name is Elvis. He is handsome, with a brown-grey tuxedo pattern and luxurious white fiber all down his long neck and chest. Over the last 12 years, Elvis and I have been the only constant in each other's lives, going through several moves, me to different homes and Elvis to different llama boarding ranches where I spent one day a week with him.

Eight years ago, Elvis was moved to an especially wonderful ranch where, at age 6, he learned to play happily with his two llama corral-mates and to fully enjoy his life. To initiate play, Elvis comically arches that long neck way back toward his tail and then suddenly rears up 11 feet into the air. And when his front feet suddenly come back to the ground, all the llamas take off running in a fun game resembling chase.

For the last three years, this happy llama trio has lived with me on my own ranch, where I can see them all day long and be with them often. For those times when Elvis and his herd don't have access to their rocky, hilly acreage, I had a rock-covered lookout and play hill constructed in the flat corral area. King of the Hill is now one of Elvis's favorite games. He sends rocks flying. Sometimes Elvis invites a corral-mate to engage in a playful round of neck wrestling. From a distance two neck-wrestling llamas can appear to be a Doctor Doolittle push-me-pull-you creature with eight legs, a thick, intertwined connecting neck, and no discernable head.

Elvis enjoys me leading him to jump over hay bales and to

walk in complex curving patterns around trees in our forest obstacle course. Elvis maintains a high level of curiousity about all things, especially about whether or not there are healthy llama treats in my pockets. Yet he waits patiently and never forces an outcome. Every day this intelligent, curious, loving, and playful llama named Elvis teaches me how to live. Looking out at Elvis enjoying simply "being" is a constant reminder for me to live life fully and to be fully present to the wonders of each moment.

~ Lana Cory Hall

Lana Cory Hall *is a prosperity coach for health, wealth, and happiness, and a metabolic balance coach. Visit her at Prosperity WithIntent.com or e-mail her at Info@ProsperityWithIntent.com.*

Puppy Teaches Self-Love

I am grateful that in 2002 a tiny, four-legged teacher bounced into my life. Chloe was my new Yellow Labrador puppy, and she showed me what real self-love looked like. The full-length mirror in my bedroom had always been my nemesis. Each trip past it triggered instant self-scrutiny. Like a frog I once saw on Animal Planet who flung out its tongue and snatched a bug so fast I couldn't see it happen until it had been replayed in slow motion, my mind would fling out tiny lashes of judgment so fast I couldn't see how they diminished me: "I look fat." "Bad hair day." "New wrinkles." One day Chloe noticed herself in the mirror for the first time. Her reaction was simple. She paused, gave her little face a quick lick, right on the mirror, and walked on. I was stunned. With one quick lick of her puppy tongue, Chloe had caused the frog tongue in my mind to be replayed in slow motion. For the first time, I saw how to stop rejecting myself. Chloe's puppy mind had no self-rejection; she met herself with the same open-hearted love and acceptance she offered to everyone, unconditionally. Now I could, too.

~ Martia Nelson

Martia Nelson, *life coach and author of* Coming Home: The Return to True Self, *guides professionals into richer, more joyful lives. For a free gift, visit MartiaNelson.com.*

My Hairball Professor

Mindfulness is the psychological practice of being completely attentive to the present moment. It involves being consciously aware of one's own thoughts, feelings, sensations, and behaviors, without making judgments. Mindfulness is a useful quality for dealing with many personal psychological issues. My Hairball Professor taught me mindfulness. Watching my cat, it occurred to me that he did not try to be other than "cat." He did what was present at the moment for him to do: sleep, eat, watch, work (prowl), or play. Yesterday was gone; there were no tears. The future held no fear. When he came to an obstacle, he went around, crawled under, jumped over, or turned back. Intuition guided his movements. At an unfamiliar sound, he listened to, investigated, or ignored it. Wanting affection, he rubbed against the object of his attention. His comings and goings were timely. His energy was conserved by satisfying curiosity and watching his surroundings with studied detachment. Observing my Hairball Professor taught me that ruminating over the past or worrying about the future wasted time and energy. It is essential is to be present to each moment and to respond intuitively. He modeled mindfulness effortlessly, without words, by simply being "cat."

~ Patricia Medeiros

Patricia Medeiros *encourages personal growth in children, adults, couples, and families. A counselor, speaker, educator, spiritual advisor, and author, she is at Patricia@WordFromTheHeart.com.*

My Best Backyard Buddies

I love animals, especially the small and precious red squirrels who inhabit our backyard. I've observed several generations over the years and look forward to their cute little babies every spring. Fiercely independent, quick, funny, and full of their distinctive personalities, they've brought me hours of joy and laughter as I've watched their crazy antics. From pulling insulation out of the attic for their nests to carrying away large apples and corncobs many times their size, they never cease to amaze me with their energy and creativity. In summer, we gather black walnuts, acorns, and chestnuts to feed them through the snowy winter, although they engage in their own rigorous nut gathering. At Christmastime, we set out a small stocking filled with acorns to include them in the holiday cheer. We talk about them as family, and I'm always concerned with their well-being. I truly love my little friends. They've taught me much:

Be determined—no matter what.

Go for the goal (the nut) and be focused.

Every day is a gift, so jump around and be happy.

Take time to relax; you don't always need to search for nuts.

Enjoy today—it's all you have!

~ Tara Kachaturoff

Tara Kachaturoff *is an online business manager and host of Michigan Entrepreneur TV. A Southern California native, she resides in Birmingham, Mich. Find her at Twitter.com/TaraKachaturoff.*

Baby Grackle Lessons

My young son and his friend found two baby grackles in our yard. I entered the scene too late to prevent contact, so we became responsible for them. We called on the local naturalist, who whipped up baby grackle food for us to feed them. She offered to keep us supplied as long as needed. We fixed up an old aquarium with sticks, leaves, and some soft clothes inside the house for these new-comers to our family. We named them D.J. and Charlie. We used a chopstick tip to feed them mouthfuls of food, and droppers to serve them water. Very soon D.J. and Charlie needed to fly, so we took them outside. Not knowing what would happen, we watched in amazement as they perched on the lilac bush by the porch door, calling insistently to be fed. Eventually the "every two hour" feedings lessened. Hungry from unsuccessful food forays, they would return to us, and we would rejoice that they were still alive.

Sadly, these valiant grackles died too soon. Caring for them increased my respect for wild creatures. I am grateful for the responsibility, our commitment and adaptability, and the connection and trust we shared. They touched our hearts and changed our lives.

~ Carol B. Gailey

Carol B. Gailey, *a licensed spiritual healer, facilitates healing and wholeness using tuning forks aligned to the ancient Solfeggio frequencies. You can find her at Facebook.com/Carol.Gailey528.*

Eye of the Beholder

I learned about beauty from a plain, cinnamon-colored cat named Zoe. When I agreed to take Zoe as a kitten, I was already quite enamored with my other cat, Emily, an elegant Angora. Short-haired Zoe wasn't my idea of a pretty cat. Emily liked being an only cat and pushed Zoe around whenever she could. Even when Zoe grew larger, Emily still dominated her. Zoe never gave up. She slept beside me every night, though further from my face than Emily. She purred in my lap while Emily crowded my chin. I knew I was falling for Zoe when I cheered the day she finally smacked Emily back. Zoe developed diabetes, and I had to give her insulin injections. She never fought me, purred when I petted her after her shots, and kept snuggling in my lap every evening. Zoe lived her 11 years with such dignified trust and unflagging optimism that she took my breath away. On her last day, I finally realized how profoundly beautiful she was. I continued to appreciate Emily's physical beauty, as I do the beauty of certain people, but now I value more the beauty of spirit I first saw in Zoe.

~ Patricia Drury Sidman

Patricia Drury Sidman *believes in love. She is a professional relationship coach who helps people find and keep loving relationships. Reach her at PatriciaSidman.com.*

God Bless America

My cup runneth over for gratitude for America, a therapy dog who lives with Ann Deavers of San Diego. Ann and America volunteer in the third grade class my daughter teaches. America has been attending third grade all year, and I expect *her* to start reading any minute. She's had many stories and books read to her. She doesn't fidget, squirm, or get unfocused. She listens! My daughter, Mindy, put out a call for help last August. Ann and America signed up—and help is exactly what they've done. Showing up consistently week after week has given these struggling readers something to look forward to and count on—someone who hasn't given up on them. Everyone wants to read to America, is on their best behavior when she arrives, and is eager to share stories they've written and words they've learned to read. The kids really revere this dog. Since America can't go across America, can a therapy dog in your community find a way into your local classrooms? The children and teachers would be ever so grateful! My daughter and I certainly are. In years to come, the children of Room 32 will recall with affection and gratitude their memories of reading to America. God bless her!

~ Sue Sweeney Crum

Sue Sweeney Crum *is a public speaker, author, and trainer in the organizing and home staging industry. Visit her at theREDteam. com or SueCrum.com.*

Lifelong Friends

We can tell the character of people by the company they keep, and we can tell what kind of life they have led by the animals they have adopted. My life included:

Feeding the deer by hand when I was about 6 years old.

Watching the cat have her first batch of kittens, and my mare have her first foal, knowing that if they could do it, I could too—and I did, one week later with the exact same ease and speed as they did!

Having my horse come back to me and wait for me to get back on after I had fallen off.

Watching my very small "hardly" dog protect my oldest daughter from an intruder.

Winning my first three-day event.

Hearing the frogs croaking each spring in the pond.

Winning the gold medal for endurance riding.

Walking up to alpacas for the first time and being told that I was the first person who ever walked up to them and got them to respond.

"Christmas Eve," who came to me after my children left home.

Gratitude does not begin to express the blessings and joy with which I have been gifted during my life.

~ Anne Ryan

Anne Ryan *is a "country girl." She uses her knowledge of animals in her coaching practice. Find Anne Ryan, coach at Facebook. com.*

Toby

Never Pass Up Opportunities

It was a warm and breezy, a perfect beach-weather day. Toby and I were scampering in and out of the surf, chasing each other around like a couple of kids, when it happened again: "Awwwwwww…" My spunky, 8-pound Morkie stopped short, a small arch of sand spraying out to the left. He frantically snapped his head from side to side, ears held high, as if to say, "Who said that?" He scrutinized everyone within talking distance, trying to figure out which fabulous person released the universal expression for "look at that adorable little dog." He locked eyes with the suspects and, without hesitation, took off full steam ahead in their direction. He *knew* they wanted to meet him, and I knew there was no stopping him! He was on a mission. He was on his way to meet the wonderful people who thought he was equally wonderful. I admire Toby's self-confidence. I'm thankful for my little bundle of love and energy, who reminds me daily never to pass up an opportunity to meet new people, to have fun in everything I do, and to be confident in who I am and what I have to offer the world.

~ *Shelly Lodes*

Shelly Lodes *specializes in helping Bed & Breakfast owners worldwide fill their rooms. Shelly travels extensively with her dog, Toby. Learn more about their travels at TrippinWithToby.com.*

Up from the Ashes

My heart stopped and did a free-fall down to my feet. Things seemed to be happening in slow motion. The Pit Bull came out of nowhere—up from the canyon. He had Phoenix by the neck and was starting to shake him from side to side in his big, powerful jaws. I saw the fear in Phoenix's eyes and felt it spread throughout my entire body, yet I could not move.

I saw my mother out of my peripheral vision. She was moving toward our white, button-nosed Malti-Poo with amazing speed and simultaneously pulling back his leash. She managed to startle the Pit Bull and scooped the whimpering, terrified Phoenix out of what surely would have been the jaws of death. I found my feet and moved toward the Pit Bull with a ferocity I didn't know I had. These actions were enough to get the Pit Bull to open his mouth enough to free our precious boy.

Phoenix is back to his former self—his running, playing, loving, energetic, sweet self. He is again interested in the world. He has confirmed some life lessons I have been working on: Let the past be the past, and let the present be a present.

~ Nikki L. Goodman

Nikki L. Goodman *owns an online business (MyVintageDiamondRings.com) and is passionate about loving animals.*

Trevor, Our Wonder Dog

Trevor came to us as a newborn. He joined a family of 11 kids, tots through teens, plus our parents. Trevor was pretty, noble, part Beagle, part other breeds, and part human. He played football with the kids and meant business. He could catch touchdown passes with the flair of an NFL star, and he did not like to lose. He jumped, blocked, and tackled with enthusiasm. *Lessons learned: Show enthusiasm, learn the skills, get down to business. Show a little flair.*

Trevor played baseball, but could not bat. However, he could scoop up ground balls, run the bases with glee, and cheer on the team. *Lessons learned: Find your place. Do your best. Cheer!*

Trevor followed the family to school. "Trevor is here!" was a frequent shout on the playground. He "guarded" the baby of the family around strangers and relinquished his post when all was well. When someone was ill, Trevor stayed at his or her side. *Lessons learned: Take care of your people and be there for them.*

Trevor made the cover of the local Sunday magazine. A photographer followed him for hours and miles. *Lessons learned: You never know when fame will come. Be ready!*

~ Trish Ostroski

Trish Ostroski *is a hypnotherapist ("Sleep with Me and Wake Up Your Life") and a writer, speaker, and memory trainer from Los Angeles. Contact Trish@RainbowHypno.com.*

Life Lessons

I had been without a horse in my life for more then 10 years before Digger, a gorgeous Palomino Quarter Horse gelding with a laundry list of physical ailments and deep-seated trust issues, was offered to me. Digger's luck was almost as impressive as his conformational flaws. He was rescued at least twice, that I know of, from certain death by kindhearted individuals who saw in his imperfect form a bright, inquisitive personality who just wanted a safe place to belong. I believe that Digger came into my life to give me a chance to rediscover who I am and how to be *me* again. I am convinced that all the animals that have come into my life have brought with them life lessons that I needed to learn. In some cases they carried life lessons that I didn't even *know* I needed to learn, and sometimes I was absolutely oblivious to the wellspring of knowledge each animal was presenting to me. Then there are those rare occasions when the lightbulb turns on and it all comes together in a grand moment of clarity. This was one of those moments. I rescued him, and he rescued me.

~ *Michelle Larsen*

Michelle Larsen *lives in Santa Rosa, Calif.*

Oscar the Teacher Dog!

I am privileged to share Oscar's home. Oscar is a 5½ pound Maltese. He allows five cats, my husband, and me to share his space. He runs the house according to his schedule and routine, but never hesitates to take a break for a chicken treat and is ready to go for a ride whenever we say "bye-bye the car." He is intelligent, loves to play, and has a contagious attitude toward life. Of course, he's beautiful. As my momma always said, "Pretty is as pretty does." And he knows how to do pretty! Oscar is my teacher, my coach, and my mentor all rolled up into one little package. He has taught me that simple things can be just as fantastic or better than expensive things. He doesn't care that I traded down when I bought my last car. He is as happy in a basic hotel room as he is in a luxury suite. Oscar also taught me about love—pure, unconditional, nonjudgmental love. That's a beautiful lesson to learn. He taught me that there's *always* a reason to wiggle with happiness. Oscar is always there for me on the good days and the great days. With Oscar in my life, there are no bad days!

~ *Sylvia Myers*

Sylvia Myers *is a virtual assistant who loves working with Infusionsoft while in the company of Oscar. You can find her at SylviaMyers.com.*

"Never" Means "Just Kidding"

I was "never":
Getting another dog.
Selling my Corvette. (Certainly not for a dog!)
Having more kids.

We had raised two awesome daughters, four Basset Hounds, and many cats. We were free. Then our daughter got married. My husband moped about our empty nest until I surprised him with the English Bulldog he'd always wanted. I never expected to fall in love, but Stella changed our lives and perspectives instantly. When she outgrew the Corvette, we gladly bought an SUV. Two weeks later, we became guardians to our niece and nephew, completing the trifecta: dog, SUV, kids. The lessons are endless: "good restaurant" now means dog-friendly patio versus good wine list. Suddenly Stella was running our lives—and brilliantly. Tuning into "Stella's Silent Wisdom" has helped us to:

Embrace life's unexpected adventures.

Be patient with humans.

Communicate silently with our eyes.

Saunter, stop, smell, breathe.

Welcome strangers with curiosity.

Take risks. (She didn't know Bulldogs can't swim.)

Strive—to be the person Stella thinks we are.

Find humor. We have, with our second bulldog, Amazing Grace.

"Never" really does mean "just kidding"! Why not? And for that, we are grateful.

~ Susan Ross

Susan Ross *is a certified Business Mastermind Coach, speaker, and facilitator who helps clients master their possibilities with calm, assertive leadership at BlueOceanCoaching.com.*

Dog Wisdom

One of the greatest things we learned from our two German Shepherds happened at their passing after 13 wonderful years. Scotty was the enthusiastic one, Benny the worrier who made sure everything was running by the rules. Suffering from cancer, Benny slowly got sicker, then Scotty suddenly fell ill and passed within a single week. We were devastated, but Scotty, unable to eat and feeling too uncomfortable to lift himself from his bed, found the strength to put on his "happy clown" face and play the joker. "It's fine," he seemed to say. "I'll bound on ahead, as I always have, and explore the mysterious world beyond the veil." And so he passed, his enthusiasm undimmed. Then Benny, grumpy at times in his youth, transformed into a smiling, wise soul, who comforted us in our loss and kept our spirits up until we could look back on Scotty's life with gladness and gratitude for his unending joy at the worst of times. Benny left us comforted, consoled, and with an insight into death that cannot be spoken, but is nonetheless precious for being a secret shared by two humans and two wise and wonderful dogs.

~ *Ron House*

Ron House *is an author in computing, wild bird communication, ethics, and philosophy, and co-discoverer of the Principle of Goodness. Find him at Ron@PeaceLegacy.org.*

Stray Angel

It was almost 20 years ago when I first encountered Indian. He was a gorgeous red Chow, but most couldn't see that through his filthy, matted fur. He was left abandoned and made his home in the fast food restaurant parking lot. I never saw him beg—he was afraid of people—but he was smart and hung out where there was plenty to eat. I was not a real "dog person," but something about this animal stole my heart. I would stop by every evening to see him, carrying with me healthy dog food, water, and bones. After a lifetime of abuse, Indian was reluctant to come near. I was consistent and showed up to our nightly visits, patiently allowing him to get to know me on his terms. It was a back-and-forth dance of forward and retreat as a connection was made between our hearts. Some might say he was just a dog—a dirty, unwanted stray. I say he was an angel, sent just for me, to teach me lessons in trust and compassion.

~ Kathy "HiKath" Preston

Kathy "HiKath" Preston *lives in Atlanta, Ga. and would like to share her life with an allergy-free Standard Poodle. Her e-mail is HiKath.Preston@gmail.com.*

Quiet Bliss

I'm grateful for moments of quiet bliss with my dog, Rincon. Especially the game of Apple. On summer evenings I pick an apple from the tree in our backyard, bite off a piece, and throw it across the yard. Rincon tears after it. While he's gobbling up that piece, I take a quick bite for myself. Then I throw the next piece to the other side of the yard, and Rincon is a streak of Yellow Labrador lightning flashing in that direction. And so the game goes. I get roughly every other piece while Rincon zigzags his way across the yard, chasing down his share. When the game is over, we are both beaming. In Apple, there is nothing happening but beauty and fun. It's the simple stuff: the apple is juicy, the grass is green, the sky is sunset-y. A running dog is gorgeous and fluid—and a running dog you love is over-the-moon beautiful. Nothing is happening outside the game of Apple and the tiny backyard oasis that is the stadium for it—not even in my head. I am never thinking any further than the next bite. That's bliss—the quiet kind.

~ Martia Nelson

Martia Nelson, *life coach and author of* Coming Home: The Return to True Self, *guides professionals into richer, more joyful lives. For a free gift, visit MartiaNelson.com.*

Roxy: Remembering with Gratitude

Roxy's routines rolled their way into my heart. I hadn't thought that would happen when two Maine Coon cats came to live with us. Melissa, her half-sister, was the cute one. Roxy would circle the bed to my husband's side and cross the headboard to my pillow, then curl up next to my heart. Her long fur needed daily brushing, so I'd sit on the floor, Roxy circling round until she just plopped. I'd call, "Plop?" each day, and she would come running. When I sat to meditate, she would squeeze into the two or so inches between me and the arm of the couch. Once Roxy must have sensed my nervousness as I meditated before a workshop presentation, and she rested her head on my thigh. Her soulful look spoke volumes. Roxy had a gentle spirit, and when she became very sick, she drew gentleness from me, teaching me about patience and kindness. The neurological symptoms came and went, yet she purred when she could. When Roxy became agitated, I'd sit in our recliner and hold her close. My heart and breath calmed her. Caring for Roxy became my expression of gratitude for her presence in my life.

~ Edith Jaconsky-Hamersma

Edith Jaconsky-Hamersma *is also grateful for discovering the labyrinth and mindfulness practice. She runs New England workshops on these. E-mail her at Hamersmae@yahoo.com.*

Tucker

Tucker Love

It's difficult to remember life just 18 months ago, BT ("Before Tucker"). A scraggly bundle of energy, Tucker stole my heart and changed my life. What a dog! Tucker looks at me with his bright eyes and melts my heart. He snuggles close and warms my heart. He flies over the ground and makes my heart sing. He sits at attention while elderly people and small children stroke him, winning their hearts. He taught me to sit and watch more of Mother Nature's show, revived my curiosity, and increased my appreciation of everything from car rides to the tiniest morsels of food. Tucker is one giant "yes" to life. Nothing crushes his happy disposition. Big dogs may snarl, the food dish may be empty, toys may be out of reach, and his mistress may ignore his late-night sighs indicating he is ready for bed, but Tucker doesn't take these things to heart. He cocks his head, looking at the situation from a fresh angle, and proceeds to go about his busy day. Nothing stops him. I love this dog and his positive attitude. I pull out my journal and take down another life lesson.

~ Laura Westerberg

Laura Westerberg *is a life coach, healthcare professional, and dog lover in York, Pa. Find out more at LifeDesignsLaura.com.*

My Best Friend

A pair of serious brown eyes peered from the stall. His thick dark mane and white blaze made him stand out above the others. His name was Austen. Although descended from a famous racehorse, he was known up and down the East Coast as a premiere hunter/jumper. He was now just a crippled, tired, and worn-out thoroughbred in desperate need of love and special attention. To me he wasn't a broken show horse. This was the day I met my best friend, crippled with arthritis, bone spurs, and an immune disease. I knew he was bound for the auction—a.k.a. the slaughter. With every penny of savings and every ounce of time and energy I had, I nursed him back to health. Although he lost faith in people, he desperately needed me. What I didn't realize was I needed him. Over time he taught me courage and exercised endless patience with me while I learned to ride. More than that, we grew to love each other, need each other, and eventually trust each other. Today he grazes peacefully among his fellow horses. Thank you, Austen, for lovingly teaching me without judging or criticizing me, while I made endless mistakes on your back.

~ Shawna McHugh

Shawna McHugh *lives in Pennsylvania with her best friend, Austen. Pictures of her and Austen can be found on Facebook.*

Twists & Turns

Though the scientific community is still squabbling over whether or not animals truly have personalities of their own, anyone who has a pet knows better and doesn't need "irrefutable" evidence to prove it. Animals can be lazy or rambunctious, shy or aggressive, playful or regal, compassionate or nonchalant, and nearly any other trait humanity displays. Just because they don't talk doesn't mean they don't communicate, and the fact that they live simpler lives than most people doesn't mean they don't possess a complex range of emotions and behaviors as do their human counterparts. After all, no one would suggest a baby who hasn't yet learned to talk lacks feeling, intelligence, or likes and dislikes.

People who are resistant to the idea of pets are often amazed at how their lives are positively impacted by allowing themselves to experience the love and companionship animals have to offer. Once "bitten" it is not uncommon for them to become permanent animal-loving converts.

While cats and dogs remain most prevalent, the following pages serve as confirmation that all creatures—feathered, finned, scaled, and beyond—have unique personalities and are contributing joy to their human friends each and every day.

Candid Conversations with Cats

L ooking into the bright, shiny eyes of my two cuddly kitties is like seeing a reflection of pure love and understanding, speaking to me through their numerous extraordinary expressions. Yes, I'm a self-proclaimed "cat person." I am grateful they're in my life because of their undeniably sweet characteristics, like quick wit, compassion for others, and the insatiable need to create mischief whenever possible, just to name a few.

Some people think it's crazy to have conversations with your pets. Well, experience tells me my cats, Maynard and Sebastian, comprehend everything I say, even if they decide to ignore me, which happens frequently. Maynard is the vocal one. His insistence on getting his way is almost human. His most common tirades are: "I want out now!" "I'm bored," and, his favorite, "I need a massage." Lately, his request to go out really means "I will hunt down a mouse and bring it to you as a peace offering!" Sebastian, on the other hand, enjoys being a stealth kitty, only talking when he really wants attention. "Comb me now" is his favorite expression. My cats have brought great joy and warmth into my life, and for that I am ever grateful.

~ Sandy Anchondo

Sandy Anchondo is a professional interior decorator and home stager whose passion is making your design dreams a reality. You can find her at ReStyleInteriors.net.

You Make Me Smile

I am grateful that you make me smile when you:
   Ask for one more treat...
   Bunch up your blankets into a pillow...
Come trotting back, trailing your leash, after sneaking away...

Unlock your kennel door...

Unzip your soft kennel...

Disassemble your double-cam-lock kennel...

Hide your daddy's eyeglasses under your kennel...

Unzip your own suitcase...

Chew only one tab off the back of a pair of sneakers...

Line up your daddy's shoes together at the top of the stairs...

Hide the liners of our shoes under your rug...

Turn back the sheets...

Play spin and twirl and "catch me if you can" on the bed...

Snore loudly while you dream...

Wake us up in the morning with a snuggle butt...

Pitter-patter down the stairs...

Splash in the water...

Kiss the babies...

Play "hide and seek" with the toddlers...

Smear the windows...

Fling your empty water dish across the floor...

Jump in the front seat of the car until I return...

Make our guests feel like they are special...

Steal Grandma's underwear and hide them in your kennel...

Share treats with your doggie friends…
Wiggle your butt…
Smile.
You are the *best* at making me smile!

~ *Amelia Hartfelder-Johnson*

Amelia Hartfelder-Johnson, *as a "petpreneur," empowers other animal lovers to live their passion for pets. You can reach her at YourPetsView.com.*

Stanley

Bunny Love

I've always wanted a bunny. I realized this the last time I went to visit my parents and looked around my old bedroom—it was full of stuffed and ceramic bunnies. In August 2006, I adopted a bunny that had been dumped in a park. I brought home the bunny, afraid of what I had gotten myself into, thinking that if someone dropped this bunny off in a park, surely it must be a bad bunny! I took it home and named it Stanley. I had two surprises in store: Stanley turned out to be a girl, and Stanley is the bunny by which all other bunnies will be measured. Stanley is a little bossy and doesn't let anyone push her around (not even our 93-pound dog), but she's also very affectionate. She licks my ankles when I'm sitting in the living room, greets me at the front door when I come home, and snuggles on the rug with me in the middle of the night when I can't sleep. Stanley has beautiful pink eyes and soft ears, and her pure white fur sparkles in the sunshine. Actually, there was a third surprise: I found out there is no love like bunny love.

~ Marjorie Old

Marjorie Old *lives in Vista, Calif., with her husband, three rescued bunnies, four hens, and a German Shepherd dog.*

My Darling McBarker

After a miscarriage, my heart needed someone special to love. I visited the local shelter, where I fell hard and fast for a gold-and-white Siberian Husky/German Shepherd mix puppy with big brown eyes.

McBarker was the dearest friend in all the world: my pillow, my clown, my confidant, my dance partner, my partner in crime, my sing-along buddy, and my kiss-my-tears-away friend. He was a protector of kitties and a companion to our two wonderful sons.

Mick grew to 65 pounds of unbridled energy. His impulsive nature got him into all kinds of trouble, like the time he lifted his leg on our freshly cut Christmas tree. Once he was so excited to come in that he failed to notice the screen door was closed and bounded right through it.

He would sit, speak, and give his paw, but I never could get him to roll over. He'd bark for his treat when I sang the Meaty Bone song. Otherwise he would obey commands only after filing a verbal complaint in his Husky way: "roo, roo, rooooooo!"

I'm so grateful that McBarker helped me through a heartbreaking time and cheered my heart for many years.

~ *Stasia Kuntz*

Stasia Kuntz *lives happily in Paxton, Mass. with her husband and an Australian Shepherd. A proud mother and grandmother, Stasia enjoys art, writing, music, and nature.*

Spiral, the Wild Dolphin

I grew up on a farm, so my pets included turtles, frogs, farm animals, and snakes. They each taught me the power of love and opened my eyes to the variety of creatures through which this love enters our lives. I've learned it comes from every direction, including the ocean.

Spiral is a wild dolphin I met in the Bahamas. She's full of spunk and loves to swim with us. I lead spiritual retreats swimming with dolphins, and its always a joy to swim alongside Spiral. She's easy to recognize: her dorsal fin is completely missing. When people first see her, they breathe sighs of sadness. But they soon forget her deformity, for it is no handicap to her. She spins and leaps with the best of them, and she has an uncanny way of reaching into people's hearts and touching them where they need it. Recently, I went out to the sea alone. I needed quiet time to reflect, as I was grieving the loss of someone dear. Out on the beautiful Bahamian ocean, it's easy for me to surrender to a higher presence, and on that day, my heart heavy with tears, Spiral came leaping in my direction. She swam up beside my boat and looked me straight in the eye. Her invitation was irresistible; her eyes were full of life and with a twinkle of joy she said, "Life is eternal... All is well... This too shall pass... Now get in the water and play with me!" And play we did. We swam side by side, spinning around each other, blowing bubbles, and laughing. The healing power of dolphins is legendary, and I returned to the boat reborn; my trust and faith in life were restored, thanks to the help of my dear friend Spiral.

~ *Joe Noonan*

Joe Noonan *is the author of* God is Delicious *and* Whole New World of Creation. *Download his free booklet, "Joyful Living: Tips from Wild Dolphins," at JoeNoonan.com.*

They Got a Dog!

I, Mighty Samson the Cat, lived with my human family and was doing just fine until June 21, 1996. That was the day they brought home this four-footed, white-and-red-colored thing. I heard them describe it as a "Brittany Spaniel mix," whatever that was, whose name was Thor. No matter to the ilk, I knew I had to show Thor who was in charge. The humans set up old milk crates by the windows where Thor could sit and see outside without scratching up the sills. I sabotaged that idea by sprawling my long, sleek gray body the entire length of the crate whenever Thor wanted to look out at the world; he would not dare chance the sharp rebuke of my talons. One day Thor came home from a visit to the vet. He was lethargic and very sleepy. Oh no! The humans did to him what they did to me! As much as I wanted them to believe I disliked Thor, I felt for the poor guy. This was the only time I lay down next to him, offering comfort. Drugged-up Thor would never remember I was kind! I was boss in more ways than one.

~ *Peggy Lee Hanson*

Peggy Lee Hanson *mentors those who experience life-changing situations and guides them through their journey using proven strategies. You can reach Peggy at MyDreamArchitect.com.*

Welcome Home

My husband, Dave, had wanted a dog since before we met. After we got married, we moved from our small apartments into a townhouse and I promised, "Once we get a house with a yard." Then we bought a house and I promised, "Once we get the yard fenced in." Then we got a fence (which I thought would never happen) and I promised, "If the perfect situation presents itself and we can rescue a dog, okay." One January night the phone rang, and it was my college roommate, who lives in Oklahoma. She rescued a dog—a puppy of about five months, her vet guessed—but her two dogs, ages 6 and 7, weren't thrilled. The dog was a German Shepherd mixed with "something small," though her vet wasn't sure what, and she didn't care enough to pay for a doggie DNA test. "How about if I bring this dog to Dave when I come visit in April? I'll have her fixed and bring her to your house." Could a more perfect situation present itself? I can't imagine that it could, and we—and she—haven't looked back since.

~ Jodi L. Brandon

Jodi L. Brandon *is a writer/editor. She lives in New Jersey with her husband, Dave, and their dog, JoePa. Find her on Facebook and Twitter.*

Colorful Budgies, Colorful Memories

"Oh no! An-an flew away!" my mother shouted as our sky-blue budgie flew out of the open bird-cage on the balcony. She then quickly shut the cage door. Chun-chun, our greenish-yellow budgie, looked awfully alone in the cage. The first time I saw An-an and Chun-chun, they were both tiny and almost featherless. My mother had brought them home from a pet shop. As time went by, they grew into beautiful and affectionate birds who brought much fun and joy to my family. They flew around inside the house freely and playfully, did funny antics, and only hopped back into the cage when they wanted to. It was a shock when An-an flew away. Moments later, my mother spotted him in a tree. Miraculously, An-an flew down to the cage my mother was carrying and reunited with his buddy, Chun-chun, and with us. I'm grateful that An-an came back and continued to share his love with us. Although both An-an and Chun-chun are no longer with us now, their colorful presence in my childhood is a dearly cherished and appreciated memory.

~ Cherry Hsu

Cherry Hsu *helps people and animals feel healthier and happier easily. She also provides intuitive guidance to clarify direction in life. Reach her at EmbraceLite.com*

The Christmas Dog

I am not a "pet person." My husband grew up in the country and always had pets, but not in the house. When our sons requested a dog for Christmas, we both agreed that our current living situation was not conducive to owning a dog. We told our sons not to expect a dog for Christmas. A pet was not on our list of Christmas presents. But our family returned home on Christmas Eve to find a dog on our doorstep. Nobody claimed the black-and-white Boston Terrier. It appeared God heard the hearts of our sons and sent a Christmas dog. Rascal was named, fed, and loved. She changed our family. This friendly dog rode with my mother to the post office. Rascal loved to accompany my husband on his ranch rounds. She escaped from the backyard to follow the children to school. Jumping upon the cinder tile fence, Rascal walked the perimeter and made her way to recess on a regular basis. With her sanguine personality, Rascal remained our adored pet for many years. A pet changes hearts.

~ Margaret G. Holmes

Margaret G. Holmes *is an education consultant, Christian leader, author, and speaker. Contact her at MHolmes1968@att.net.*

My Canine Is Feline

Kona is clearly a dog. But don't try to convince her of that. She looks like a dog and barks like a dog, but she believes she's a cat. Having a doggie bed for Kona is almost a joke. Her comfy spot to take a snooze is on the back of the couch or under a piece of furniture. Her favorite foods are tuna, salmon, and shrimp. She looks at me rather indignantly when I put dog kibble in her bowl. Kona can curl up in a ball so tight, she shrinks to half her size. And she grooms herself all day long. Good thing, too, because she hates to be near water. Giving her a bath is a formidable challenge. No fortress is a challenge for Kona. Her cat-like agility is unsurpassed. She can take one swift leap, from a complete standstill, and perch herself on top of a fence or wall. Once she's up there, she can maneuver across with the confidence and precision of a tightrope walker. Kona is pretty persnickety, but she's also loyal, protective, and lovable. My little Jack Russell/Whippet mix is the coolest cat on the block!

~ Melanie Kissell

Melanie Kissell *shares shoestring marketing strategies with mompreneurs who want to ditch the corporate world and work from home. You can find her at MelanieKissell.com.*

Cougar:
From Psycho-Kitty to Cuddlebutt

ougar had been badly abused (skull fracture, broken tail-bone) before I got him. Friends joked that he was my jealous husband in a past life, because he hated every guy I talked to. The first time he saw my boyfriend kiss me, the cat went ballistic, jumped on his back, and slashed all the way down. Rick was a good sport about it, but the poor guy probably still has scars. Since Cougar thought he was protecting me, Rick forgave him. But he never managed to make friends with the cat.

I also had to teach Cougar how to purr—he cuddled with me at night, and I could tell he was happy, but he often looked confused, as if he was trying to remember something. I realized one night I had never heard him purr, so I made purring sounds. It took several nights, but he finally realized what he was missing—and it was louder than any purr I'd ever heard before. For 12 years after that, he curled up on my neck and purred away. In those 12 years, Cougar went from a raving psycho-kitty to the biggest cuddlebutt I've ever seen.

~ Debi Schepers

Debi Schepers *is a freelance writer and editor in Chicago with a penchant for finding and loving strange and/or damaged kitties.*

First Day

Eighteen months ago I bought my first puppy, an American Bulldog I named Storm. (She soon lived up to her name.) The breeder gave me a rag with her mother's scent on it when I brought her home to make the transition easier. The time came for me to put her in the kennel for the first time. I decorated it with a couple of toys, a soft, fuzzy blanket on the bottom, and the rag. She started to whine, and it took all of my strength to not open the kennel, scoop her in my arms, and tell her everything was okay. "Don't give in. If you give in, she will expect it and whine every time," I kept telling myself. I began to feel less guilty when I could hear the crying come to a stop—but then the whimpering began. I looked at her large kennel down the hall in my bedroom. She whimpered as she was trying to cuddle with the rag, the only scent she knew. My heart began to break, and tears streamed down my cheeks. I just felt so awful that I had to be strong and not give in. I began to wonder what was wrong with me; I had always been a strong person. I could easily watch a sad movie and not have one tear in my eye. As I calmed myself down and was able to breathe at a normal pace, I called my mother. I began to tell her what had been happening and began to sob again. To this day I still cannot talk about it without crying (and apparently, I can't even write about it, as tears are now beginning to trickle down my cheeks and my nose is beginning to run). "If this is what it's like having a dog, what the hell am I going to do when I have a child?" I asked my mother between gulps of air. She chuckled, as it was obvious that I had learned my first lesson in motherhood. It is amazing how one creature can make such an uplifting impact on a person's life. I thank Storm for giving me such a wonderful a life lesson. I know that my life would be very empty without her.

~ Jenny Whetzel

Jenny Whetzel *is writing her first novel. You can read more of her work at Paws2Smile.wordpress.com.*

Ode to My Blissypooh

I understand that most people, when writing an homage to their beloved pets, usually speak about their beautiful meow-meows or their lovable wuppie-puppies. For me, though, my heart longs for the pitter-patter of my adorable pet rat, Bliss. Unusual perhaps, but if you knew her, you, would have fallen madly in love with her too. During the darkest period of my life, reaching the deepest depths of sadness, Bliss provided me with that unconditional love I could not give myself. I was also incapable of receiving it from others, deeming myself undeserving. My soul ached for understanding, which came in fleeting moments, but the one constant was my beautiful little Earth angel, always there to provide refuge with her cuteness and outrageous antics.

One of Bliss's most amusing acts was to pry open the refrigerator door I would, at times, absentmindedly leave ajar. She was aiming for that cheese, and she always got it. (Yes, it's true: they do love the cheese.) Though I might have grown accustomed to this, my fiancé, John, friends, and family members never quite could. I actually found it rather hysterical; it was one of the few things, during that stage of my life, that drew bellows of laughter from me. Observing this petite creature time and time again, so determined to not only get that massive door open, but to then jump up three levels to get to her delicious treat was unfailingly intriguing, to say the least.

I learned so much from her about persistence. I sit with that memory, that visual of me laughing aloud with such jubilation. I now say a prayer of gratitude for having spent three wonderful years with her, the maximum life span for her species. Rats are one of the most misunderstood creatures on earth: so intelligent, so funny, each with his or her own distinct personality, and truly so so loving. I miss you, Blissypooh. I miss your whiskery kisses and treasured springtime snuggles that we cheerfully shared. May you rest in peace in cute little rodent heaven. There will never be another that could ever replace most wonderful you.

~ *Ana Maria Sanchez*

Ana Maria Sanchez, *MS, is a holistic counselor, "heal your life" educator, and Reiki healer. Find inspiration by visiting her at FreeTheLightWithin.com.*

Dude, I Am Brody*

"I am a happy-go-lucky, big lover-bear kinda 'bro.' I love my life and my peeps. I am feelin their love; all my senses are strong like me. Oakland is my hometown, and, accordin to me, the main capital of Pitbulls and bros in the world. I love bros on 'one.' They always compliment me as the best-looking Pit. We are mobbin' hella barred up, smackin' and scrapin'. I am the king of Pit bulls for sho."

"I am really grateful for my life. I was the runt of a litter of seven. When I finally popped out, my mom was too exhausted to lick me clean. I was not breathing. My human mommy took me into her front paws and gave me mouth-to-mouth. She loves me so much. I can't believe she could then hold me in one paw, and now I weigh 100-plus pounds. My daddy has a tattoo of the Bay Bridge on his chest. I want a tattoo like that on my belly to show my pride for my homies whenever I roll around. Diggitt? Holler at you later!"

~ *Marlies Janzen*

Marlies Janzen *lives in Oakland, Calif. She writes about Brody to improve the reputation of pitbulls as loving companions. Befriend her at Facebook/Marlies.Janzen.*

*Editor's Note: This piece is written in "rap style," and we curbed the grammatical and punctuation fixes we'd normally apply. You can look up unknown terms in this piece at UrbanDictionary.com. (We did!)

Bandit

Bandit

"**B**andit, where did you come from?"

It was a sunny morning and I was sitting on the porch with my coffee and my "stray cat," who I named Bandit because of her black "mask" on a white face. I spied this mystery cat out of my home office window a few months before as she was lying in a small cool patch of cement on a hot San Diego day. A softie for "tuxedos," I started providing for her.

Her name could have been "Skittish" as I gave her some water and food, which she didn't nose into until I was well out of sight. This went on for weeks and weeks. I commented to my friends, "I will never touch that cat."

But one day I put down the food and water and she came close enough that I could give her a little scratch on the head. Soon she made my front porch her home. Actually she took over the outside digs and let me know it was breakfast, second breakfast, lunch, snack, and dinner time by a tremendously loud, consistent, and yes, I'll say it, annoying yowl outside the door. Nearly every time I heard it I rolled my eyes—tell me, why did I start feeding this cat again?

Our rare peaceful morning moments, like the one with coffee and sunshine I described above, were some of the few pleasant times with Bandit. But it was always a mystery—where did she come from? How old was she? Who was her previous owner? I thought I'd start with the question that sunny morning by asking her outright, "Bandit, where did you come from?"

She didn't reply then, but it was just a few days later when a man came up my walk and Bandit ambled up to him and circled his legs. My heart started racing. Was this Bandit's owner? Was he coming to take Bandit—my cat! I love that cat!—away from me?

I darted out the door, taking a deep breath to steel myself in case I had to give her up.

"Hi," he said. "I just dropped by to see Nayla."

"Nayla? You know this cat?"

"Yes, I live a few blocks west of here. I took care of her for awhile."

"Do you know where she came from?"

"She lived next door to me with an older lady. The lady got a dog and Nayla and the dog didn't get along, so she put the cat outside. She didn't really take care of her much, though, so my wife and I started feeding her."

I decided to try to steer him away from announcing he was taking the cat back with another question.

"Do you know how old she is? My vet said at least 10."

"I'd say she's closer to 17. She's been around a long time. I see she wandered over here and seems happy with you. I just drop by once in a while to say hello to her."

"You do?" I said, thinking I never saw this man before in my life! My neighbor gave Bandit another stroke, gave me a little wave, and headed down the sidewalk once again.

I looked at his retreating back and then down at my cat saying, "Huh. I guess now I know where you came from, Bandit. I'm going to keep calling you that, by the way."

Her answer was a yowl. It was lunchtime, after all. I went in to get it with a smile.

~ Donna Kozik

Donna Kozik *lives in San Diego where she shows people how to Write a Book in a Weekend®. Find her at WriteWithDonna.com.*

Through Thick and Thin

I didn't get Macey's full story when I adopted her from the Berkeley Humane Society, but I suspect she's a dog who's had her heart broken. She wasn't used to kisses or hugs (barely tolerated them) and had trouble learning to trust people. When we had been together about 3 years, Macey had an encounter with a feral cat that left her in a lot of pain even though she'd barely been scratched. After going to multiple vets, we discovered she had a flesh-eating bacterial infection and she ended up losing all the skin underneath her belly. After staying at Advanced Critical Care in Tustin, California for over a month (thanks, Dr. Mineo!), she came home, all bandaged up and exhausted. The two of us made daily 60-mile round trips for months to get her dressings changed. And then the trips happened every other day and then every 3 days until finally, nearly a year later, she had healed. An interesting side effect of all this is that Macey learned to trust people and is a much sweeter dog, coming to me now and then and laying her head in my lap to be kissed and hugged.

~ Kim Bidwell

Kim Bidwell *is an avid runner, voracious reader, foodie, and devoted dog lover living in Southern California. Connect with her at KimOnFacebook.com.*

What Makes Me Laugh

I truly love my animals—they make me laugh every day. I have two dogs and two cats. My dogs are Jack and Jasper; Jack is a runner and Jasper is a barker. My cats are Lilly and Prix; Lilly hunts mice and Prix is lazy. Lilly and Jack are best friends. Every time Jack wants to go outside or go for a walk, Lilly is right there beside him. It is the funniest thing to see: me walking my dogs down the street and my cat following. Jasper is all of 9 pounds, much smaller than Lilly, yet he waits next to the door as I let the cats in and then pounces on them. Lilly just takes it. She sits there and waits until he's done. When he moves on to Prix, she hisses and strikes back. Prix is my lazy cat who loves to eat. When she is ready to eat she jumps off the table and walks down the stairs. She is so big you would swear that it sounds like a person walking down the stairs. My animals have such distinct personalities, and they are so much fun that they make each and every day a blast.

~ Doreen Dilger

Doreen Dilger *is a home-based business coach who empowers women to create systems to get more done daily. She can be reached at DoreenDilger.com.*

The Kitty Clan

I heard a high-pitched "meow" coming from the living room. As I turned the corner, there was a kitten. I ran to the open screen door to see another kitten being carried by his ear and meowing, "OWWWWWaaaaa! Momma, put me down!" All I could do was watch. Methodically, Momma brought her kittens into my living room, then moved them and herself behind the couch. *Yikes!* Four-week-old kittens! This wonderful blessing, which we called "the Kitty Clan," brought the cat count to a whopping nine: two senior cats, Puffy and Mocha; Sparta, a kitten from Momma's previous litter; and the Clan. It was quickly determined that names were in order. A friend said, "Once you name them, they're yours!" To which I replied, "What am I supposed to do? Call them Tabby 1 and 2, and the black ones Fluffy, Medium Fluffy, and Extra Fluffy?" Instead, they were named Braveheart, Sissy, Patches, Charcoal, and Hoss.

This blessing was financially and emotionally enormous. Finding homes for the Clan was difficult and heart-wrenching. However I am now called "Godmother" by the Clan's new parents, a role that I take very seriously. We kept Hoss and Braveheart. Momma decided that being feral again was bliss. She was spayed prior to returning to her blissful lifestyle, and she says "hi" to us regularly. I learned that a blessing is an opportunity to learn more about loving. The Clan taught me unconditional love and devotion. Being given the opportunity to participate in their growth was magnificently beautiful. They cemented my conviction that we all need a good home, and that giving up on that by takng the easy route was not the purpose of this blessing. The biggest lesson? Blessings breed blessings.

~ Carol Lynn Fletcher

Carol Lynn Fletcher *is a writer, intuitive, graphic designer, and virtual assistant in the San Francisco Bay Area. You can reach her at FletcherBiz.com.*

The Entertainer

Entertaining—that's an understatement. Ever since the day Simba, my handsome, loveable red tabby, entered my life it has been anything but boring. Simba routinely jumps on the bed in the middle of the night. One particular night, Simba had been exploring the inner workings of the fireplace. I opened my eyes to discover his white belly and paws covered in soot, and so was my white comforter. As I lay there in disbelief I wondered how in the world he managed to pry open the fireplace glass doors—and whether this was going to be a frequent occurrence. Luckily, Simba moved on to the kitchen. He loves exploring the kitchen cabinets, so I decided to designate one kitchen cabinet "all things Simba." Occasionally, I have discovered Simba's Ziploc bag of treats scattered all over the kitchen floor. What amazes me is his ability to open the bag. I just wish he would learn how to clean up after himself. (There's always hope.) Each day Simba continues to amaze me with his talents. I am forever grateful for the joy that he has brought into my life, and I could not have asked for a more amazing companion.

~ *Joan S. Epstein*

Joan S. Epstein *is a green living coach. You can reach her at InspireGreenLiving.com.*

My Cat Mentors

My rescue and healing crusade for cats began late one night during a severe thunderstorm 10 years ago. Awakened by the loud screeching of newborn kitties, I decided to venture out in the rain, into the jungle-like backyard of my new home. I picked up two little tiny creatures, abandoned by their mother. They fit comfortably in the palm of my hand; so fragile, yet desperate not to drown as their brother had. From that moment I was hooked! Little did I know that this discovery would not only impact my life, but also redirect my work in the years ahead. What followed is just a fairy tale. The house and backyard turned into a nursery, a hospital, and a university, all at once. So many animals—cats, raccoons, opossums, etc.—showed up daily: hungry, wounded, or ill. All were welcomed, fed, and treated. Those with debilitating conditions, such as poor immune systems and kidney, heart, or digestive issues, opened a window of opportunity for me to become a "natural" pet healer, after most conventional protocols failed them.

Two of my beloved cats, Chato and Plomo, were given early death sentences at a very young age due to their weaknesses. I wasted no time using my own personal natural approach to self-healing. They both lived for many more years, I'm happy to report. They received and accepted my help with gratitude and love. Who could ever imagine how these animals can take over our lives with unconditional love and gratitude? Their displays of love and affection have yet to be surpassed by humans, in my experience. Words can't describe my eternal gratitude toward all of them for touching my life so profoundly, both spiritually and emotionally. No wonder the Egyptians worshipped the cat: beauty, love, wisdom, joy, and peace are just a few of the rewards they bring to us. I dedicate this piece to my "cat mentors": Snuggles, Chato, Plomo, Pepo, Lola, and Luna, the ones who give me a reason and a purpose to continue my lifelong animal healing journey. I am proud to be able to manifest and portray the hidden beauty of our four-legged friends.

~ Cecilia Matthews

Cecilia Matthews *uncovered the power of our bodies to heal themselves. She helps people and animals heal naturally and quickly. Contact her at Ceniga@bellsouth.net.*

Hit the Showers

Summertime is a wonderful time of year…especially the summer before your freshman year of college. It's a time of excitement, anticipation, and plenty of parties.

After arriving home late one evening from yet another summer bonfire, I couldn't help but notice a strange "funk" in my room. I really didn't think much of it, though, after all I was an 18-year-old guy—of course there was a strange funk in my room. So I stripped down to my boxers and rolled into bed, excited at the prospect of sleeping in the next morning. As it turns out, the next morning would have to wait, because halfway into my back roll I discovered why there was a funk in my room. My parents' new kitten (we'll call him Mr. Whiskers) had mistaken my comforter for the litter box…and Mr. Whiskers had the stomach flu.

It's hard to describe the feeling of rolling into a puddle of cat diarrhea late on a warm summer night, but suffice to say, it was not pleasant. After the initial shock and subsequent horror, I collected myself long enough to clean off my back, wad up the comforter, and throw it into the hallway.

I was tired. I needed to sleep. I would deal with Mr. Whiskers in the morning.

Unfortunately, Mr. Whiskers couldn't leave well enough alone. Early the next morning I was awoken by the still-unfamiliar call of a young kitten. Ballsy, if you ask me, or maybe just naïve—either way, I was not having any of it. After carefully ushering Mr. Whiskers out of my room, I nodded back off to sleep.

However, 20 minutes later, my world changed forever.

That's because 20 minutes later I was awoken again. *This* time, by a soft sprinkle of liquid.

Warm, yellowish liquid.

On my face.

To call that moment a low point in my life might not be totally accurate, but it might not be that far off either. In the battle for feline respect, I was losing—badly. Nothing to do at that point but crawl into the shower and weep.

Mr. Whiskers two. John zero.

~ *John Weisbarth*

John Weisbarth *is an Emmy-Award-winning sports reporter and TV host from San Diego. He is also the winner of the Golden Mike Award and the San Diego Press Club Award.*

I Love Little Baby Ducks

A boy who grows up on a farm in the country carries a memory stocked with pet stories: happy stories, funny stories, and some tragic stories. I still remember the day our newly hatched ducklings arrived in the mail. Twenty-five peeping little ducklings peered up at me, my five brothers, and my baby sister as we lifted the splintered lid off of the small wooden crate. They lived in a large pine box in the garage. Above the box was a heat lamp to warm these recently orphaned ducks. My brother Eric and I used to wait until the ducklings were all nestled down, sleeping in the circle where the lamp's heat gave the most concentrated warmth. Then we would quietly grab the lamp and move it to another area of the box. Then we waited. The creeping coldness caused the ducks to fidget. Something should be said about sleeping baby ducks: they sleep in piles, a collage of wings, beaks, and yellow fuzz all mixed together. Eventually one of them would wake up shaking from the cold. Slowly opening his eyes, he'd spy the circle of light across the crate. He'd panic and flap his wings, all the while jumping up and down on the heads of the others around him. A few seconds later he would start to race toward the light. The commotion awoke all the other ducks. Within a minute or two, the entire slumber party had relocated and was once again fast asleep under the light. Eric and I would let go of the light and watch it swing like a pendulum until it returned to its original position, and the duckling evacuation would start again.

As the ducks grew, they yearned for the open sea. We

knew this from the mess they made splashing in their water bowl, a favorite pasttime. When the ducklings were ready to begin swimming lessons, we found an old plastic tub that fit in the crate perfectly, leaving plenty of space around it for those who just wanted to sunbathe. We constructed a wooden ramp up to the pool and into the water. The ramp allowed the ducks to visit the tub as often as they liked. More importantly, however, the ramp was submerged an inch or two in the water so the ducks could get out of the pool and over the plastic rim that encircled the tub. The pool addition worked out great for several days. At any given time, the pool had 10 or 15 ducks circling on the water's surface.

Each morning before we left for school, we peeked in on our ducks to make sure they had dry newspaper on the floor and fresh water. One morning, as we approached the duck's crate, our eyes focused on the tub. The wooden ramp had been knocked down. Four drowned ducks floated motionless on the still water. The previous night's swimming party had ended in tragedy. Apparently some clumsy duck kicked the ramp down on his way to bed. The accident hit us hard. Those poor little ducks swimming, and swimming, and swimming, until finally exhaustion swept over them along with the pool's dirty water. We took the dearly departed ducklings and disposed of them on the roof of our barn. There their bodies decayed next to the remains of the victims of the infamous chicken massacre of '82, the numerous kitten plagues of the late '70s, and hundreds of rat-poisoned rodents.

The time came, or so we thought, that the ducks were old enough to make it on their own. We scooped them all up into their mailing crate and walked back to our pond behind the barns. As soon as we released them, they bobbled toward the water. We set an old metal and wood barrel on its side to provide them with a home to nest in, and left them with plenty of duck food. After school the following day, we rushed back to the pond to visit the ducklings. Not a trace of them could be found. Not a trace ever was.

~ *Daniel Kriley*

Daniel Kriley *grew up on a farm in Herman, Pa. and is a high school theatre teacher in San Diego. Find him at Facebook.com/ Daniel.Kriley.*

Animal Accolades

The following pages are filled not only with accolades for the critters that have come and gone, but for those that continue to add depth and enjoyment to the lives of their humans.

Anyone who has loved knows one is never able to fully prepare for the loss of a loved one, and a beloved pet is no exception. However long one is graced with the love and affection of furry companions, saying goodbye to them is never easy. But knowing they will one day part ways is not enough to stop most from embracing the joy to be shared.

Life and love are inclusive of chance—but most would agree that the benefits always outweigh the risks.

Many have found comfort in the following poem. The author remains unknown—but was clearly someone who knew the love of a four-legged friend.

The Rainbow Bridge

Just this side of heaven is a place called Rainbow Bridge.

When an animal dies that has been especially close to someone here, that pet goes to Rainbow Bridge.
There are meadows and hills for all of our special friends so they can run and play together.
There is plenty of food, water and sunshine, and our friends are warm and comfortable.

All the animals who had been ill and old are restored to health and vigor; those who were hurt or maimed are made whole and strong again, just as we remember them in our dreams of days and times gone by.

The animals are happy and content, except for one small thing; they each miss someone very special to them, who had to be left behind.

They all run and play together, but the day comes when one suddenly stops and looks into the distance. His bright eyes are intent; his eager body quivers. Suddenly he begins to run from the group, flying over the green grass, his legs carrying him faster and faster.

You have been spotted, and when you and your special friend finally meet, you cling together in joyous reunion, never to be parted again. The happy kisses rain upon your face; your hands again caress the beloved head, and you look once more into the trusting eyes of your pet, so long gone from your life but never absent from your heart.

Then you cross Rainbow Bridge together....

~*Author unknown*

More Than I Expected

I clearly remember the moment I met Spikealicious. I looked into a carrier of five 3-week-old kittens, and he was front and center, silently hissing and stomping on his tiny paws. I laughed, thinking to myself, "What a brave little one, but I'm not buying your act!" I wasn't one to believe in love at first sight until that moment. I named him Spike because of his bravery, but that didn't fully describe his personality. He was larger than life. He was so sweet, he was delicious. So he became Spikealicious. At 8 weeks old, Spike was diagnosed with a severe heart defect. Veterinarians told me, "Don't get attached to this one. He won't live to see his first birthday." "Too late," I thought.

At a year old, Spike underwent a life-saving surgery funded by the generosity of strangers. For six years, he enjoyed a trouble-free life. He saw the veterinarian more often than most cats, but somehow Spike enjoyed those times, too. He had a way of getting in your heart and taking hold of it. By no means was this something you would accept begrudgingly. When Spike loved you, he loved you with his whole being. He worked his magic on everyone he met, which worked to his advantage—and mine at times, as veterinarians and technicians were under his spell in no time. He received extra TLC. I was comforted in knowing that those caring for him knew he was special.

Life became challenging and, honestly, quite scary when Spike was 6. My little Spike spent days at a time under his blanket in an oxygen chamber. He scared the bejesus out of all of his human family on several occasions. He brushed off each scare, hurdling them one after the next, knowing there was something greater to live for. My Spikealicious passed on February 5, 2010, at 2:05 a.m. There were moments during his transition I wished it were me and not him. I wanted to help him, but knew I needed to let him go. I prayed that he would have no physical memory of his final moments. My belief that the soul exits the body before death occurs, to protect it from experiencing pain, helped me let Spikey go. Although I had hoped for more time, what we had was more than I expected. I will always be grateful for every second.

~ Kerry A. See

Kerry A. See *is a pet-care business owner, Reiki practitioner, animal rescuer, pet product designer, baker, gardener, and aspiring writer. Contact her at RufflyPurrfect.com.*

Our Golden Angel

People often remark to us that they wish they could live a dog's life. A life filled with playing, eating, sleeping, and begging for more loving! Heck, even our daughter Jill has told us that she wants to come back and live the life that our Merlin has! Merlin Ari LoveJoy, our angel in a Golden Retriever's body, has been a wonderful gift in our lives and is a constant and consistent energy to help create more Love and more Joy in every moment of every day. With his tail wagging, head tilting to one side, and that adoring face that only puppies and children seem to have, he creates magic. It is a magical wisdom that our angel dog, Merlin, inspires in everyone he meets. This magical wisdom is a tribute to the bond of dog to man. Did you know that dog spelled backward is God? Yup, that is the best reminder anyone can have to share in more Love and Joy. Merlin is our constant reminder to live in Love and Joy! May you all live with Love and Joy with your pets. They are precious; cherish their time on this earth with you.

~ Richard and Trisha LoveJoy

Richard and Trisha LoveJoy *are Small Business Consultants and Certified Professional Success Coaches who inspire clients to live their dreams. Contact them at ANewLeafCo@gmail.com.*

Fella

A Furry Kind of Love

Fella was simply the best furry companion we ever had. He was a gray, short-haired cat with black stripes and expressive green eyes. On cold winter nights, he would circle around, waiting for us to sit down so he could jump on our laps and curl up. He liked our warmth, and we liked his warmth. We found comfort in this furry little creature sleeping on our laps. Sometimes he would lie on my lap with both paws up on my chest and look lovingly into my eyes.

I called him our Fur Factory. When he got scared, he jumped straight up in the air and landed in the same spot, releasing a cloud of fur into the air. You could actually see the shower of fur descending to the floor. Our other cat, Chessie, had long, gray fur. She also lost a lot of fur. Once in a while, especially after Fella had been frightened, I'd find a piece of gray fur with a black stripe in the middle—a Fella Fur.

After about 19 years, Fella started to decline. I agonized over having the vet put him down, but I didn't know how much longer I could endure seeing his decline. As much as it hurt me to think of it, I told my husband one day that if he was still with us when we got home from work, we might have to take him to the vet. I nervously entered the house after work. My husband got home a couple of hours before I did. Fella left us just 30 minutes before I got home that day. What a gift Fella had given me to spare me that decision. I mourned the loss of Fella, but comforted myself with the pleasant memories of his companionship.

Fella is still with me in my heart, and he reminds me of that every so often. I've heard that cat fur can linger in a residence for years. One day about six months after Fella was gone, I found a gray fur with a black stripe in the middle. It happens more rarely now, but I still occasionally find a little striped Fella Fur someplace in my house or on a piece of clothing. I'm so grateful for Fella's companionship and his trail of striped furs. Every fur is precious.

~ *Susan Brownell*

Susan Brownell *is passionate about writing and cancer caregivers. Her award-winning website supports cancer caregivers when they need help most. Find her at SanctuaryForCancerCaregivers.com.*

My Big Fast Red Ferrari

In the fall of 1993, following unexpected changes, intense decisions, and life challenges, I was inspired to seriously hunt for a horse again. After owning a number of wonderful horses, delivering two foals, breeding a mare from Montana, and riding as a young girl, I longed to return to the world of kissing velvet noses, smelling barn aromas, and gliding bareback in the sand—moving as one on the clouds through the wind. That is when I met Overlook Ferrari, who, over the next 18 years, became my best friend, soul lover, spiritual advisor, exercise trainer, and teacher of life lessons. My "big baby boy" stood 16.2 hands, with his sorrel red chestnut coat shining like a copper penny in the summer sun. He was a clown, a genius, a guardian, a loner, a free spirit, and a feisty friend. With Arabian tail held high, his elegance and regal presence presided as he became known as the older, wiser leader of the herd; thus, the nickname "King Ferrari" was born.

Dearest Overlook Ferrari,

You opened my heart, supported my soul, and filled my world with joy. There is no separation. We will fly again. With loving gratitude forever, your mom,

Amy

~ *Amy E. Kelsall*

Amy E. Kelsall, *PhD, is an executive/leadership/development coach. She also directs communication and HR Master's degree programs for working adults. Reach her at Amy.Kelsall@du.edu.*

Baby's Story

Bab was her name and, from the first time I visited my friend, Bab would come, lie at my feet, and purr. She was 8 months old then. Bab has only three full legs, due to a mishap at birth. She's a beautiful orange with lots of white patches. My friend moved, leaving her behind. Bab was going to be put out on the street. That was the beginning of our life together, when she was a year old, weighed only five pounds, and had a small meow like a baby. Hence her name became Baby. Now she's 3 and a great companion, content to follow me everywhere, including the bathroom. Baby meets me at the door when I arrive home each day and greets me when I wake up. She's adorable. She shows her displeasure by turning her back on me and limping away slowly for sympathy. When she is playing and running about, one would never know that she only has three legs. She runs up and down the stairs just like any other cat. I love her dearly, and our relationship is unique. Baby gives me love bites as if I am her mother. I truly don't know what I would do without her now.

~ Sharon G. Teed

Sharon G. Teed *has been an inspiring writer since she retired. She lives in Toronto, Canada, and can be contacted via e-mail at Sharon.Teed@sympatico.ca.*

A Letter to Benji

Benji, my Spirit Dog,

You gave so much and taught so many lessons. You accepted everyone and never complained. You let everyone you met draw comfort, warmth, and calmness from you. You loved doggy life, chasing the cats, teasing the fish, hiding your bones, dancing with me in the living room, and rolling in the grass amongst the wildflowers in the nearby field. You especially liked taking trips to the dump, sitting on my lap while trying to steer the car. But most of all you liked hiking and riding in your backpack when you tired. Everyone wanted to hold you or carry you. And who could blame them? You were so cute you even made the front page of the local newspaper, and as a result, got caught by the dog officer for not being licensed. Oops!

As gentle as you were, you were also strong, tough, and brave. You never whimpered at the vet and never yelped at the groomer. You took needles and baths with grace even though you didn't like either. Walking with you was always a challenge. You had to stop and water every tree and twig to mark your spot. And you had many spots!

My special times with you were when we climbed mountains to pick blueberries and when you curled up beside me in bed. You were just a little round ball of fur leaning into my waist. When Tasha, the little "white tornado," joined our family, the whole tone of the house changed because of her energetic playfulness and lack of discipline. But, as always, you accepted her, never became jealous, played tug-of-war with her, and slept side-by-side with her. You were a real gentleman when you shared your toys and food dish with her. In true Benji style, you even tolerated her when you weren't feeling well.

Benji, you have been my little man and I love you. Thank you for giving me so much, even the little kiss on the cheek (you weren't a kissy dog) the day before we had to say good-bye. I then knew you were telling me it was okay to release your spirit. You are "Spirit Dog." Eat lots of heavenly bones, play with angelic toys, run around in the green grass of doggy heaven, and lift your leg to salute your new home.

Love,

Mom

(Note: This letter was read at Benji's funeral with many tears.)

~ Karen J. McCarthy

Karen J. McCarthy *is a Reiki Master living in Maine. She provides Reiki treatments for people and pets. She is a lover of all animals.*

No Mask for Harley

Harley, a wonderful yellow Labrador Retriever, is an important part of our family. He entertains us every day with his own special habits. Harley never tries to hide his feelings and doesn't get embarrassed; there's no "mask" to hide anything for this dog. Harley finds amusement everywhere—from doorstops to sticks, to any type of dog toy. When he gets really excited, he does a "wild dog" routine where he spins in circles and just acts goofy. Harley doesn't care what anyone thinks; he just has fun. He is also a creature of habit. If you change his routine (or if there's a different person working at the front desk of the veterinarian's office), he lets you know that he's not happy about the disruption. But as long as you have a dog treat in your pocket, Harley is still your friend. We have learned much from Harley and are grateful to have him in our lives.

~ *Beth Sponseller*

Beth Sponseller *loves animals and helps pet owners provide optimal nutrition for their furry friends. You can reach her at NutritionForCritters.com.*

Olivia

Tribute to Olivia

My Dear Sweet Girl,

Although you only touched my life for a few short years, your contributions were profound. Through your traumatic story as a rescue dog from the mountains of north Georgia, to your life in the Arizona desert, everyone will soon know what the life of a "bait" dog is like. Helpless, homeless, and unloved, you came to me as a beam of light, teacher, healer, and messenger dog. Your love, affection, and relentless connection to me has changed my life forever. My heart now holds a special place for all rescue dogs, and especially all "bait" dogs. Your message will be heard throughout the world so that other dogs will not have to endure the life you led before coming to live with me. My tribute to you is work to rid the world of the blood sport of dog-baiting. Your message will be heard. You trusted me when you trusted no other. Love prevails, Olivia. Thank you for coming into my life. I will always miss you, but I know that you are watching from above.

~ *Lynne M. McCarthy*

Lynne M. McCarthy, *ASID, is an interior designer, author, and intuitive reader. She specializes in designing environments for dogs. Find out more at zDogz.com.*

My Furry Love Ball

He just showed up, literally on my doorstep, a voyager I thought, because the word *stray* didn't seem to fit that tiny gray-and-white fur ball with big ears. I couldn't bear to hear him cry, so in he came, at least for the night. After a can of tuna, he curled up contentedly on my shoulder and purred himself and me to sleep. I awoke to see the charming heart-shaped marking on his head and his beautiful green eyes gazing lovingly into mine. Busy with college and work, I had never realized something was missing from my life, but at that moment I knew it had been Sinbad. Since my landlord did not allow pets, I offered to pay "rent" for him. Our building then became "no pets, except Sinbad." He quickly became a combination son and best friend. When we play fought together, ironically I wore a dog hand puppet. Of course I always let him win. I can still imagine his warm cheek gently nuzzling mine. Sinbad, my beautiful boy, thank you for 11 love-filled years.

~ *Helen M. Thamm*

Helen M. Thamm, *APRN, CPC, is a career success coach, creator of NurseCareerSuccess.com, and author of* How to Manage With a Magic Wand.

Fred

Fred was a mutt—a 65-pound sable-and-white Lab mix. Fred took responsibility for keeping everything dangerous away from "his people," such as leaves, snow, and the neighbor's cat. When he heard fireworks or thunder, he hid under the bed, which was no small feat considering his size. When the doorbell rang, Fred barked ferociously, lunging and baring his teeth to protect us from the unknown. When I answered the door, he hid under the bed. When my sons got rambunctious and ran around, Fred hid under the bed. One time I forgot about a loaf of frozen bread left on the counter. The next day, I went into the laundry room and found the chewed up bread bag on the floor. I held up the bag and asked, "Did you do this?" Fred put his ears down and did a walk of shame. He hid under the bed.

When I went to bed each night, Fred squeezed under the bed directly beneath me. We both felt safe and protected. Fred shared 10 years of my adult life, good and bad. No matter what happened, Fred was always there—usually under the bed. I still miss that soft snore.

~ *Susan Veach*

Susan Veach *is a graphic designer from Southampton, Pa. She is a bibliophile, traveler, art lover, gardener, mother, and wife. Reach her at SusanVeach.com.*

Biscuit

My Clutch Poodle

Biscuit was just the right size—the perfect companion. Because I always carried him tucked like a clutch purse under my arm and propped on my hip, a friend called him the "Clutch Poodle." Biscuit enjoyed riding shotgun, lazing around, and scavenging sweets, especially chocolate. As a puppy, Biscuit was attacked by the dog next door. This attack resulted in lifelong internal injuries, so his mischievous behavior was often excused. Despite his injuries, he took his job of guarding the house very seriously—from under the bed! I'm grateful for Biscuit's unconditional love. We miss his sashay of a walk, his quiet begging, and his soft brown eyes. He was beloved.

~ Melisse Campbell

Melisse Campbell *is an artist and purveyor of antiques who photographs, paints, writes, and designs. Her work has been featured in national publications. Visit MelisseCampbell.com.*

A True Love Story

She was beautiful—black and brown, with a posture filled with a pride and grace that very few believed a Dachshund could have. Her name was Nickan, and when I made my entrance in the autumn of 1965 she had already been in the family for a few months. My mother quickly learned that if I was crying she just had to put the little dog in my crib; when Nickan licked my feet, I became calm again. We were companions for almost 16 years, and during that time she was the sole being that gave me the neverending consolation of always being there, always understanding. She ran away from home a few times, and on one horrendous occasion she was stolen from outside the supermarket, but she always managed to find her way back home.

The last days of her life were awful. She was unconscious on a thick blanket in my parents' room, and we took turns caring for her. When she finally let go, the grief almost tore my heart into pieces. But today my heart is filled with gratitude. Nickan, thank you for being the first love of my life.

~ *Kicki Pallin Serby*

Kicki Pallin Serby *worked as a radio host for Swedish radio for many years. She now studies sustainability in Uppsala, Sweden. Find her at Twitter.com/KickiPS.*

His Name Was Lucky

Someone had thrown this darling kitten out a car window, clipping off part of his tail, and he hadn't been adopted. He was just waiting for us. Our granddaughter and I decided to give him a new name. I wanted Ziggy, and she wanted Wiggles (he likes to dance), so we named him Ziggle. Ziggle acts like a polished gentleman. He loves to lead the way when walking from room to room. He's so affectionate, and he loves to hold hands! If my hands are anywhere near him, he places his paw on me as though to say, "Aren't we wonderful together?" And, while hard to believe, he caresses my face with his paws and draws me near to lick my nose. I sometimes wonder if we were partners in another life. Ziggle loves to lay on my husband's upper chest, snuggling along his neck. It's heartwarming to hear Ty chuckle in delight. I take cues from Ziggle, too. If someone visits and Ziggle doesn't come around, I know the person isn't likely to be invited back. Ziggle is our guardian and friend, and our lives are more blessed and fulfilled since he came to live with us.

~ Diana Garber

Diana Garber *is changing the world one business, one home, one person at a time. This Master Feng Shui Practitioner can be found at IntuitiveConcepts.com.*

Gunny

For the Love of Gunny

The first time I met Gunny (short for Gunnery Sergeant) I made the mistake of opening my car door inside the parameters of his invisible fence. I was immediately attacked—but not in the way you might expect from a 100-pound dog. There was no malice. No baring of teeth. No growl or low rumble. It was all tongue. All tail. Wagging and licking, his entire body one gyrating mass of joy and spirit, Gunny had come to say "hello." It was the beginning of a beautiful relationship that lasted more than 10 years.

Gunny looked more like a black bear than a Labrador Retriever, with a huge head I'm convinced had to be that large in order to hold the enormity of his personality, his curiosity, his intelligence, his quirkiness, and his capacity to love. His heart was equally as big. His left eye had a slight "droop" to the bottom of it, the result of a congenital defect that kept him from being a show dog or top breeding dog even though his papa was one, but to me it was that "defect" that gave him his charm, and it's what continually enabled him to trick us into giving him one more treat or one more piece of whatever we happened to have on our plate.

Gunny lived for two things: to hunt and to eat. I'm not sure which one was more important to him. In the duck blind, he was all business. Focused. Body tense and on point, waiting for the whistle that sent him darting off at full speed to retrieve. He was an amazingly strong swimmer, with a stubborn streak that wouldn't let him quit until he had brought back his prize. Back in the blind with his mission accomplished, he'd fall asleep with as much speed as he showed just minutes earlier in the water.

And when he wasn't hunting, he was eating. And sleeping. And dreaming of eating. I never knew a dog more in love with food! There was nothing he wouldn't eat (except broccoli), and no amount was ever enough. When, at the age of 12, he lost that passion for food, we knew it was time to say goodbye. We had to put our beloved, sweet friend to rest this past December, and our world lost a little of its brightness that day and every day since.

~ Evelyn Kalinosky

Evelyn Kalinosky *is a speaker, author, and executive coach who mentors businesswomen to achieve a more sacred kind of success. Visit her at EvelynKalinosky.com.*

A Blessing in Our Life

On Saturday, July 3, Stephanie and I were thinking about a "big" way to celebrate Independence Day. We decided that freeing a dog from a cage would fit the bill, so we headed to the animal rescue shelter. As we walked down the rows of cages, several dogs barked loudly, and many charged the front of the cages. We then passed a cage where a 6-year-old Beagle named Toby was quietly sitting in the back corner. He looked frightened, but when I bent down to the cage, Toby cautiously approached. He was gentle and quiet, and we learned that he'd been abandoned twice before. Our hearts melted at the sight of his sweet face, soft floppy ears, and quiet demeanor. Toby seemed perfect, and we took him home. Luckily, it turns out that Toby enjoys sitting on the couch and early bedtimes as much as we do, and he's even learned to love kayaking! Toby is truly a member of our family. We set out on July 3 to bring happiness and independence to a dog, and in the end it is our hearts that have grown larger and more full of love! Thanks, Toby, for being the perfect dog for these empty-nesters.

~ *Jim Palmer*

Jim Palmer *is known internationally as "The Newsletter Guru" and author of* The Magic of Newsletter Marketing *and* Stick Like Glue! *Learn more at NewsletterGuru.TV.*

Jake

For the Love of Jake

"I love these cats, but in a year, we're getting a dog," my husband said. A year and a day later, my husband announced, "It's time to get a dog." My protesting that "the extra day makes that null and void" didn't stop him from taking me to meet Jake. I knew what an English Springer Spaniel looked like from the photo of my husband's beloved childhood dog in Scotland, but I didn't recall *that much hair.* And—hey, wait!—I didn't recall agreeing to definitely get a dog (damn those subliminal wedding vows). Apparently, Jake had been adopted, briefly, with his sister. He'd been returned to the shelter, still not groomed. I asked, "What happened to their first family?" "Decided to travel." "Where's his sister?" "Second family kept her, but returned him." "So, if we adopt Jake and have to return him, it would be his third strike, meaning potential doom?" "Yes, but he's perfect for you. He'll be fine with cats." Hmm…"perfect for you and fine with cats." I recall thinking that about my husband, and had read that same line in an e-mail someone named Candy at a rescue league had sent to him. "Are your shelter and my husband in cahoots with Candy? Is that her real name?" I asked. "Yes." "Can we do behavior tests now?" "Yes." Jake's score was perfect, but that third-strike rule still worried me. My husband proclaimed, "Jake just chose us!" I felt Jake building a bridge between the fear in my head and the knowing in my heart. The third-strike rule was exactly why we had to adopt him, not the reason we shouldn't.

Eight years later, on our anniversary, our beloved Jake crossed the Rainbow Bridge. I cherish memories of perfect antics, perfect naps, and the maddeningly perfect way he caught a ball just once, right after we declared "Jake can't catch a ball." I'm grateful for the love of Jake and for learning a few important things:

You can be both a "cat person" and a "dog person."

The right dog can bridge time and geography between childhood and adulthood.

It's okay to trust your husband with a woman named Candy.

You can walk proudly and appreciate the exercise, even in Wellies and a reflective vest, and carrying poop bags.

I can slow down.

There's always time for belly rubs.

Strangers who learn dogs' names before each other's aren't crazy; they're letting the dogs build a bridge.

~ Beth Duerr Munro

Beth Duerr Munro *specializes in combining coaching and organizing to help people clear the clutter from their hearts, minds, and spaces. Visit her at DefineYourSuccess.com.*

With Love from Kannik

L ast week we learned that our dog, Kannik, had an inoperable tumor. In a few days, our 12-year-old Alaskan Malamute changed from an energetic dog into a shell of her former self. Although she was running a month ago, by last Thursday she was no longer able to stand. Watching her fail was heart-wrenching, and we made the difficult decision to help her. In the moment of her death, I held her and whispered my love into her ear, as I have done so many times over the years. Her long, white fur smelled like a wool sweater. She was comfortable in my arms, and her warm, brown-eyed gaze was calm and content. There wasn't time to think between the moment she was here and the next when she was gone. In the blink of an eye she was no longer with us. As her body relaxed, I was left holding onto a part of her that was no longer whole. Instantly I missed her and felt the tearing pain that comes from having to say goodbye. She is gone now, but my memories remain. I will always cherish the time I had with my beautiful Kannik.

~ Kelli O'Brien Corasanti

Kelli O'Brien Corasanti *is an author, personal trainer, life transformation coach, business owner, and mom who lives in upstate New York. Find her at FindingMyWayBackToMe.com.*

Azza

Azza

She came into my life at a time when I must have needed her most. I say "must have needed" because I really didn't believe, at that time, I needed her at all. I was busy with school, work, and my own chaotic life, and I didn't want to take on any more responsibility. But I did, and she is Azza: Azza, my sweet pea! My heart! My sweet-za! She has been there for me since the day I saw her in the kennel at the humane society, and she will be there for me until her body goes. She makes me laugh, smile, and cry. I am grateful to have her in my life. I appreciate the joy she gives me. I appreciate her everything—her stubbornness, craziness, and silliness. She is my peace. Without her, who knows where I might be. She keeps me on track, and I need that. Being responsible for her is helping me stabilize my life. I really needed her, and for her I am grateful!

~ Bonnie Baker

Bonnie Baker *is an outdoor enthusiast enjoying the ride of life! She loves the ocean, music, her dog, and spending time with family and friends.*

I Want a Gray Cat

66 "I want a gray cat. And I'm going to name it Foggy."

I'm not sure the exact day I made this announcement to myself and to the world—I think I was a teenager— but I do remember when I was ready to make it happen for real.

My long-time calico cat "Bart" had passed on and I was ready to get a new feline companion. Or two.

I started asking around "I'm ready for a new cat—where should I go?" Friends suggested shelters, vets' offices and online classified ads. I took note and said I'd check them out, but didn't get around to it for a few weeks because of some trips I was taking that would mean I'd be away from home. For sure I wanted to be there to give special attention to my new cat. (Or two.)

As I was driving home from the last one—a short vacation in Las Vegas—I thought, "It's time. I'm going to get that gray cat. And I'm going to name it Foggy."

Even before I lugged my suitcase in the house, I turned on the computer and downloaded a few hundred email messages. One from my friend Patti—who I hadn't heard from in years and years—jumped out at me. The subject line: Cats in need of a home.

I opened the e-mail, which she had just sent an hour or so before, and scrolled down to see the pictures. The second one was a gray cat! I called her up and left a message, "I want the gray cat. And the gray cat's best buddy."

She called me back the next day saying that the gray cat was popular and several people had asked about him, but, luckily, I was the first. I went over that night to meet him and his "best buddy," and a few days later Foggy and Felina came home with me—both small enough that they could sit on my chest, and I barely knew they were there.

I definitely know they are around now! Foggy's favorite "game" is to swat at pens, especially those that are in use. Felina is the picture of cuteness napping on the cable box and is a rare cat indeed as she loves to have her belly rubbed.

These two kittens-turned-cats have brought me many hours of joy and companionship. I'm grateful to have Foggy and Felina in my life!

~ *Donna Kozik*

Donna Kozik *lives in San Diego where she shows people how to Write a Book in a Weekend®. Visit WriteWithDonna.com.*

Tales of Eternal Love

When it comes to being grateful for my four-legged children, there aren't words to express the depth of my feeling. There are several entries in this book that will attempt to express that love; from me, a tribute. Growing up, we were forever rescuing animals: dogs, cats, hawks, birds, even squirrels and chipmunks were found, nurtured back to health, and either kept or set free, depending on their species. As I think back to each family member, tears of both joy and sadness come for those loved and passed. There were:

Peppy, my Toy Poodle who had been abused by her former owner and would bring me her puppies to care for.

Jason, a half-Shepherd, half-Great Dane who would pull his doghouse around the yard, drink beer with my dad, and greet me when I returned home from grade school through college.

Kitty, who saw me through a horrible breakup and three moves, and graciously accepted all her new siblings when I bought them home.

Reggie, my beloved Shitzhu who loved absolutely everyone and whom I bought at a yard sale.

Henry, our orange tabby who had lived at Burger King and had had most of his bones broken before we rescued him. He lovingly followed my husband around the yard like a devoted puppy.

Miss Missy, the most beautiful calico cat, who would initiate her new siblings into the household by giving them a sound thumping.

And many more, whom I loved just as much and who will always hold a special place in my heart. I thank God daily for the seven children who continue to brighten my every day: Sasha, Sheba, Buddy, Eggie, Junior, Toby, and Jasper. They continue to teach me about life and love.

~ *Sandra Martini*

Sandra Martini, *dogpreneur, business and marketing mentor, truth-even-when-it-hurts-teller, raw foodie, and devoted friend, can be found with a dog under her desk at SandraMartini.com.*

Prince

A True Friend

I am grateful for a dog called Prince who touched my life; I will never forget him. Prince was a German Shepherd with a big heart, born in South Africa in 1996. He lived in South Africa around the time that Nelson Mandela was president. One of the fun things that Prince really enjoyed was swimming in a local pond, retrieving sticks that were thrown for him. He was a confident swimmer. His only dislikes were a provocative yapping Poodle trying to get under our fence, and on one occasion a cat who must have been watching too many *Rambo* movies, as he attacked Prince while he was being walked. Needless to say, Prince put the cat in its place, and it never challenged him again.

Prince moved with us to a town just outside London in 2000. Prince was a loving German Shepherd who also seemed powerful and intimidating to some. He never harmed any adult, child, or animal. Our children used to climb all over him, yet he did not even growl when they were rough with him. He was sweet-natured, affectionate, and intelligent. He brought much joy to my family. Toward the end of 2009, my family and I moved to the countryside, to an area of outstanding natural beauty, great for dog-walking, cycling, and walking. Prince did not come with us, as he died unexpectedly. We really missed him. Almost a year later, another dog, called Louie, came into our lives. He is from a animal shelter and he is also a very loving dog who makes us smile. But we will always remember our beautiful dog called Prince. He was a true and loyal friend to the end.

~ Melanie G. Robinson

Melanie G. Robinson *is a wife, mother, infopreneur, and generally good person—a lover of animals who is passionate about family and friends.*

My Loyal Friend Rusty

Our dog, Rusty, has been our loving companion for 15½ years. He is a sweet, mild-mannered friend who is slowing down physically, but he still does his best to show his affection and loyalty. When I look at him, I see the Cocker Spaniel puppy we found at the animal shelter who paced along the inside of the enclosure looking pleadingly at us for acceptance. I see the young dog who frolicked on walks and loved to chase the tennis balls we threw for him. He would jump up on the bed and snuggle with us, wanting nothing more than to be close, be loved, and share his affection. I see the shameless beggar looking at the treat cabinet and at us alternately until we rewarded him for his endless optimism. Rusty can't jump up anymore, so he finds familiar places to sleep and walk, where his failing eyesight doesn't hold him back. I am so grateful to have enjoyed his company these many years. When it is his time to depart, it will leave a hole in my heart that will be difficult to fill.

~ *Douglas Brennecke*

Douglas Brennecke *is a San Diego mortgage originator who listens to his clients, educates them, and tells them the truth. Reach him at DougBrennecke.com.*

Little Black Kitty

Buka, my cat, is the reason I am writing here today. She helped me through one of the toughest times in my life. We had a crisis pregnancy in 2001; our baby girl was placed in a loving home via open adoption. Then along came Buka, born in May of the same year. She was abandoned, and I remember someone saying that since I already had two cats, I should be strong like I was with our baby girl and give this cat to the shelter. Those words helped me keep this wonderful little black kitty. She was very small and she was very smelly, but she was my muse. After the adoption, she helped my healing process. Buka was always right there, ready to snuggle. She came running anytime she heard me crying, even when I was silent. Sadly, she passed away in October 2008. I miss her every day! I would like to take this opportunity to thank her for being in my life, for helping me heal, for being a big inspiration, and for helping me become the writer I am today!

~ Melody Heath-Smith

Melody Heath-Smith *is a married mother of one. As an aspiring children's book creator, she is writing a "phantasmagorical" story. Contact her at MelodyTheWriter@hotmail.com.*

A Precious Gift

When my mother was 85, she had to stop driving. She was heartbroken, as she was fiercely independent, doing her own errands and going on shopping sprees. My brother and I decided a Siamese kitten would be the "purrfect" gift to lift her spirits. Mom was thrilled with her new kitten named Precious. He was creamy white with black points and bright blue eyes. Extremely affectionate, Precious followed Mom all over the house. She played with him, she watched TV with him, and he would jump on her shoulder when she did the dishes. Precious's purrs, rubs, and snuggles made Mom happier now that she had her companion. Several months later, Mom was diagnosed with brain cancer. With home hospice and caregivers, Mom was able to spend the last few months of her life at home with Precious. Precious's engaging personality charmed everyone: the hospice nurse, the caregivers, and Mom's many visitors. When Mom passed away, I became the proud "godmother" to Precious. He is a special cat, and I am so grateful for the joy and affection he brought to Mom during her last year on Earth. It is an honor to be the guardian of this precious gift, Precious!

~ *Kathy Lyons*

Kathy Lyons *is an animal minister, writer, speaker, and cat artist. She enjoys spending time with her two cats, Precious and Raggedy Andy.*

Daisy

Daisy's Love

I vividly remember the day I met my Daisy. She was a 4-month-old stray puppy, and from her distinct features it was clear that she was part Pit Bull. I was gathering my things from my Jeep when I looked up to see her charging at me. I was alone, with no other humans anywhere in sight, and there was no time to seek shelter. As she got to my feet, she literally flopped over on her back, paws up in the air, and smiled as if to say, "Just love me, because I already love you." And I have loved her since that moment. Daisy's love has been such a blessing—not only to me, but to every person she meets. She is so full of love. In fact, she has so much love that my husband and I share her with the world! We take her practically everywhere—nursing homes, schools, community events, local businesses, parks, and parades—and everyone greets her with open arms just as she greets them with an open heart. What a wonderful message she has for the world: *everyone* deserves to be loved. And for that, I am grateful.

~ **Rhonda Chuyka**

Rhonda Chuyka *teaches high school chemistry and jazzercise in West Virginia, was named "Teacher of the Year" in 2009 and 2011, and lives to inspire others.*

My Thanksgiving Day Gift

Our "little darling" Schatzi —the most precocious puppy in the litter—came home on Thanksgiving Day and immediately began to heal our hearts, broken from the passing of another faithful friend. Full of confidence and pizzazz, Schatzi won the hearts of the judges as she strutted her stuff. She quickly became a champion, but, in turn, she set the agenda for me to become the champion of her purpose—living for the welfare of pets and strengthening the bond to their families.

Together, we taught puppy classes. Schatzi filled in so that both husband and wife had a puppy to teach. She acted as though she never learned a thing from week to week, to optimize the "treat machine" as she offered up her cutest behaviors. Together, we interacted with the next generation by going to school events to entertain the young and to inspire teenagers considering pet careers. Together, we visited the nursing home to lift the spirits of pet lovers who just wanted to run their fingers through her long, silky fur and slip her a cookie or two from their food trays as they talked about the pets who had meant so much to them. Together as business partners, we make the pet-sitting rounds. Other dogs look forward to playtime with her while their pet parents are out of town.

Together, we explored possible sites for a proposed dog park. High windy fields, an old rifle range, and other parcels of land were ruled out. Prime land was posted with "No Dogs Allowed" signs, but we held on to the belief that the best site would become available. Together, we "woofie wooed" ("whoo hoo" in dog talk) when the Frostburg Dog Park finally opened for unleashed dogs to run, play, and show off their agility skills. Together, we raise funds for homeless pets. Schatzi entertains children at our booth while I speak with their parents.

Together, we form friendships with holistic veterinarians so that every facet of her healthcare is carefully evaluated. I have embraced techniques that once seemed "out there," as Schatzi benefits from them. Together, we live in the moment as we blog about life from Your Pets View—passionate pets raising the passion within you! I truly appreciate my pet— my Thanksgiving gift—for I see the best in her. She sees what your own dog sees in you: the best!

~ Amelia Hartfelder-Johnson

Amelia Hartfelder-Johnson, *as a "petpreneur," empowers other animal lovers to live their passion for pets. You can reach her at YourPetsView.com.*

Pucca

Being Pucca

Hello, mankind! My name is Pucca. I am a ferocious black miniature Schnauzer who lives to serve my master, Isabella. She is the most beautiful and tender-hearted of your species. Since I was a puppy, she has taken special care of me and has given me preferred treatment. For example, she lets me sleep on the bed when her parents aren't home; she also hugs me about 100 times per day and constantly tells me she loves me and that I'm beautiful. She feeds me nutritious food, and, when adults are not looking, spoils me with human food treats. For these reasons and more, I have taken an oath to protect her and to play with her every day for the rest of my life. I train hard to achieve superior speed, strength, and agility so I can succeed.

Every morning I help Isabella get ready for school. While I do this, my assistant, Lulu, a Shih Tzu, wakes up Isabella's father, Frank. Lulu has discovered that the best way to do this is by licking his feet! All three of us board the moving cage, which they call "car," and take her to school. I sniff for dangerous scents the entire way to school, growling at anything that smells or looks suspicious. Sometimes I bark for no reason at all, just to make Isabella feel protected. Other times my superior sniffing detects an unfinished candy under the seat, which I promptly consume.

Upon returning home, I stand guard by the window and keep an eye on the house, barking at every person in sight. At 1:45 I begin to wag my tail to signal that it's time to pick up Isabella. If this doesn't work, I scratch the front door and bark until I get attention. When Isabella gets in the car, I am the first to greet her and the first to be greeted. I can tell she misses me as much as I miss her. As soon as Isabella and her family sit at the table to eat dinner, I respectfully step outside to stand guard. Sometimes, however, I lie underneath the table very quietly, especially if they are eating Spanish rice (my favorite). Isabella's little brother, Frankie, is an expert at dropping rice on the floor. I have no problem with this behavior, and I don't mind helping to clean it up.

Instead of helping Isabella with her homework, I let her parents help her while I rest from the long trips to and from school (plus I'm really not good at math). Finally, the last thing on my list before going to sleep is to make sure that she showers and puts on her pajamas. She normally takes a bath, so I sit next to her the entire time. Isabella is the best master a dog can have. I'm the luckiest dog in the world. She always talks to me and makes me feel loved. I'm happy to be her dog, and I want her to know that I will always be there for her and that I love her too.

~ Frank Nunez

Frank Nunez *and Claudia Beltran del Rio are proud parents and dog owners who understand the importance of the relationship between children and pets.*

No Pacemaker Required

Bandit is our mascot. Tennis is our game. We serve up kindness with Kids Play For Good, acing causes on courts in your backyard and mine. No cause is too big to conquer. Our hearts are stoked by kindness, while our shots are filled with sting. Caring is our armor; it's the sweetest coat of all. We raise our racquets high. Chasing tails and poaching dreams, Bandit leads our champions' team. And like Bandit, we play in the moment to stay in the moment.

Joy is our favorite ball, quick-start tennis our winning format. Mushers for causes nationwide, we make our mark. Pulling together we are top dogs. Playing with heart. Kids at the start. Doing great work. No napping, no yapping. Passion flies our net. Made in America. Made with heart. Serving up the stuff of champions. Bandit stole our hearts, and he'll heal your heart. After all, he's the only service dog taking center court! Kids Play For Good: not for the faint of heart, only for the big of heart.

Bandit is our mascot. Service is our creed. Kindness is our rallying cry. Do you want to join our winning team?

~ *Lynn Morrell*

Lynn Morrell *helps tennis kids nationwide champion kindness and hone their philanthropic muscle online and on court. Visit KidsPlayForGood.org.*

There She Was

I remember the first time I saw her. She was sitting underneath a citrus tree in our backyard. It was a cold, rainy afternoon, and there was sadness in her eyes. We didn't know where she came from, but she had been visiting our backyard on a regular basis. One day, when my mum came home, she discovered that there were three kittens sunbathing on the grass. They had been hiding in our basement for weeks. The cat who came into our backyard had given birth to these three lovely kittens, and she needed our help looking after them. We gave them a home. Gentle, affectionate Mila has been living with us for about seven years now. I'm very thankful for her sweet companionship and joy over the years. She brought comfort to my family when my dad passed away over a year ago. Thanks, Mila, for the cuddles and smooches. Thanks for the gifts ("pizza" and "sausages") that you left at our doorway. We love and adore you!!

~ *Cynthia Hsu*

Cynthia Hsu *is a designer who loves animals. She works at EmbraceLite, helping people and animals heal. You can reach her at EmbraceLite.com.*

Eat, Play, Love

Our 9-year-old black-and-white cat named Lowee ("Low-we") is a great teacher of life lessons in our home. She came to us by way of our veterinarian in Charleston, who had rescued her as a tiny stray. I wasn't really looking for another kitten, as we already had three at the time, but this little ball of energy caught my eye. When I called my husband regarding this new addition, he said, "Yes." I replied, "Great, honey!" before he had a chance to change his mind, and Lowee was ours! Since that time Lowee has become the cat that cuddles when we need comfort, plays with imaginary objects when we need entertainment, and grabs kibbles from her sisters (Megan, Misha, and Cattie) when we need to be reminded that sharing is something that takes a little practice. She also tends to act like a puppy dog, so we often call her "Lowee Pup." She follows us around the house as if to say, "Hey, what are we going to do next?"—almost wagging her tail! She is always ready to see us when we arrive home and is the first in bed at night, ready for snuggling. We love *all* of our cats, but "Lowee Pup" is definitely the most interactive. She keeps us energized and reminds us that life is better when you remember to eat, play, and love!

~ **Susan Douglas**

Susan Douglas, *MD, is a psychiatrist, mother, friend, daughter, entrepreneur, and founder of the No Mommy's Perfect website. Learn more at SusanDouglasMD.com and NoMommysPerfect.com.*

Lupey

Lupey:
My First Wolf, My Companion, and My Best Friend

Our adventures together began when Lupey was but a 4-week-old muscular bundle of fur. I was called to the Whipsnade Zoo outside of London, England. Two smiling animal caretakers stood by Lupey's crate, challenging me to reach inside and retrieve him. I counted the fingers on my hand, wondering how many would come out. At first I could not find him, but in the back corner was this wonderful 7-pound creature. Our life together had begun.

I took him to Cambridge where I was a research student at the time. After the first night, Lupey snuggled on my pillow with me at night and followed me around during the day, wagging his tail. Our favorite game was his version of rugby. The first time we played, when he was about 3 months old, he popped the ball in his now-powerful jaws. He then dropped the flattened ball at my feet, waiting for me to pick it up. I did and tried to run past him. Down I went, with his jaws on my pant leg. Then it was his turn. I could never catch him, even when he slowed down or stopped a few feet away. Zoom, he was gone.

We moved to a farm with a wonderful landlady who also loved him. There, Lupey played with the dogs and chased playfully after the horses. From England we traveled together on the Queen Elizabeth to New York. I drove him to my parents' home in Potomac, Maryland, and then to Rochester,

New York. Our daily romps together continued.

Next stop was the University of Oregon, where I took my first academic job. Lupey was the hit of the campus. People begged to see my friend. We got two female companions for Lupey, and he sired his first pups, digging a den and guarding it carefully. Although he grew cautious, he remained friendly to me, never once threatening or biting me. I loved him.

Our last stop together was in Nova Scotia, Canada. After a happy 11-year life Lupey passed away, and I cried. My friend was gone. Later, I worked on lifetime development with about 50 wolves, but there was never another Lupey. Now I am finally writing a book about my friend.

~*John Fentress*

John Fentress *is a world-recognized scientist who also loves nature. This entry is about his dearest friend ever, Lupey. Read and enjoy.*

The Magic of Animals

There is no question that animals are attuned to many things that escape the attention of humans—didn't Lassie always know when Timmy was down the well? Many owners believe their pets actually have a sixth sense and know when earthquakes and significant weather changes are going to occur. Perhaps they are able to detect electrical and atmospheric changes or subtle shifts in vibrations and frequencies.

Researchers will readily attribute some things to an animal's heightened sense of smell—making it possible for some dogs to anticipate seizures and detect certain cancers or a drop in blood sugar levels. Many even believe they know when another animal or a human companion is on the brink of death.

Humans may never understand why some animals seem to know when bad news is on the way or to sense when extra compassion and concern are in order, and yet many pet lovers have experienced those exact things.

Even if science could offer a tangible explanation, true animal lovers need no further evidence to accept that their furry companions just seem to know some things that their people don't. The special bond between humans and their animals is not contingent on their unique ability to sense subtle changes or know when trouble is lurking—those are just a couple of the sometimes mysterious bonuses that come with these incomparable relationships.

What Is a Pet?

What is a pet? Some would say it is a tamed or domesticated animal. Others would comment that a pet is an animal that is usually affectionately cared for that often plays the role of a companion.

A child may be referred to as a teacher's pet. Indeed most anyone who is especially cherished or favored is often referred to as a pet. Adults frequently have pet names for their loved ones as a demonstration of fondness and affection.

To me, a pet means all of the above and so much more. When I think about the dogs, cats, hamsters, gerbils, birds, and even fish that have inhabited my home, I feel the love, companionship, and camaraderie that we shared. I have happy memories, funny pictures, and a great reason to get up in the morning. I get to start my day in gratitude for the unconditional love I receive just for showing up, being me, and sharing my time, attention, and some morsels of food. My pets have provided so much for me that mere words pale in their description of how grateful I feel for them. What is a pet? To me, everything!

~ *Monika Huppertz*

Monika Huppertz *asks, "Are you ready to remove obstacles and leave your restrictive life behind? Step towards your success with purpose and passion!" Learn more at LivingYourTruth.me.*

Her Name Means Promise

She came into my life in her old age. At first I was her pet sitter. She is a beautiful silver-coated miniature Poodle named Sheba. Her owner, Idris, had a debilitating stroke and asked me if I would take Sheba permanently. Sheba has lived a full life, starting out as a breeding dog in Texas. After Idris bought her, she entered a life of pampering and playing. It is my joy to love her through her senior years. She is blind in one eye, yet she loves to run fast across the backyard! She also is quite content to sit quietly on my lap while I read a book. It's amazing how God works in the details of our lives. My husband and I were separated, and I was feeling lonely. Sheba came to me and provided that special fur-buddy companionship. Her name means "promise," and I believe she is God's promise to me that everything is going to be okay in my life as well as in Sheba's. We are a blessing to each other. Having her happy spirit and loving presence surrounding me gives me encouragement and helps me stay positive through a difficult time.

~ *Nadine Joy Lewis*

Nadine Joy Lewis *enjoys taking care of pets in the Eagle Point, Ore. area. She can be reached at HappyDayPetSitting.com.*

A Soulful Soothing

I was newly married with a new job and new house. To my delight, I also got an adorable Chihuahua who could sing like an angel and had love in his eyes. One day, my husband worked on the car while I put a cover on the coach. My Chihuahua snuck out of the house. I searched all over for him. To my horror, he made it to the neighbor's yard and was killed by their dog. I cried for three days. My sister insisted that I get another Chihuahua—not to replace him, but to help me heal. She was right. My new puppy had a different personality, but helped heal my aching soul. Ironically, my sister passed away later, which broke my heart. I was left with her two dogs, who could not replace her but again helped to heal my aching soul. I still have her dogs and mine, and they are all truly a soothing blessing.

~ Terri L. Cunkle

Terri L. Cunkle *is a teacher, creative business owner, and writer. Find her books at Creativity101.com.*

Angel

My Happy Thought

I am grateful for when you wake me up early every morning, pawing on the blanket and nudging me with your nose.

You are so happy to see me get up and walk toward the kitchen, constantly wagging your tail as if you are the one leading me toward the treat container.

I am grateful that you never cease to welcome a day with excitement, prancing on two paws and doing circles.

I am grateful that when I arrive home you anxiously wait for the garage door to open.

I am grateful when you help yourself to the bed and that, when I call out your name, I see the blanket move up and down to your tail wagging.

Happiness in your life is all about the simple things: meal time, walks, treats, playing fetch, belly rubs, sleeping under the blankets, soaking up the sun on a cold morning, and curiously following insects in the yard. You are my daily reminder that life is really not that bad.

Most importantly, I am grateful that no matter how happy, mad, busy, sad, stressed, tired, or down I get, I will unconditionally be the best part of your day.

They say that having a pet can extend your life. I believe a pet can save it.

~ Dina Rocha

Dina Rocha emigrated from Mexico and is a UCSD graduate. She lives in San Diego with her loving family and dogs, Sammy, Jordan, and Angel.

Healing from Ginger

My fever was 101 degrees and my stomach pain was almost unbearable after a restless night at my daughter Lori's home. The next morning when Lori opened my bedroom door, in walked the family cat, Ginger. She had never paid any attention to me, and I had never noticed her much. She had always kept her distance, and to me she just was not pretty. Ginger jumped up on my bed, walked softly up on my stomach, and put her belly right on my painful spot. She lay there and looked me right in the eyes. I could hardly believe what was happening: she had come to heal me! She didn't move. She was intent on her mission. My pain became less. For the rest of the day I drifted in and out of sleep. Ginger would leave, but would come right back. I accepted her and apologized for thinking she was not pretty. Her fur actually felt like my old mouton coat I had enjoyed when I was a teen over 50 years earlier. Her dark eyes seemed to bring a quiet calmness. I shall never forget Ginger's part in my healing.

~ Annette Denton Livingston

Annette Denton Livingston, *a terminal illness survivor, shares her new book:* Living Wellness Today: One Woman's Search for Healing. *You may contact her at LivingWellnessToday.com.*

Gift of Angels

Maggie, a wild Australian magpie, was a bird on a mission. As a chick he made friends with our dogs, Scotty and Benny, along a country lane by letting them tap him on the chest. Their remarkable friendship attracted attention again months later when Maggie sought Benny's help in dealing with adversaries. After the dogs died, Maggie dispelled our sorrow by singing the sweetest songs. His melodious voice had the magical ability to just dissolve the pain in my heart. Together with his sisters, Cindy and Tammie, his beautiful songs filled the air with the most magnificent carols, and one never felt alone. Maggie's rowdy antics, superb negotiating skills, and friends from other bird species around our yard entertained us for hours. Contrary to all popular tales about magpie aggression, Maggie with his mate, Vicky, trusted us with their children, as did his foster parents, Fatty and Molly. I thank Maggie daily for open-ing our lives to the incredibly rich, loving relationships that exist among wild bird communities in the backyard, and for letting us into their extended family to share that love and awareness. I thank Scotty and Benny for gifting us this incredible legacy.

~ Gitie House

Gitie House *is a co-discoverer of the Principle of Goodness, and writes about communicating and building relationships with wild birds in the backyard at WingedHearts.org.*

The Rescue

My love and gratitude for my cat, June Moki Lani Nippo, is endless. June was the kind of cat who, when friends would come in the door and see her for the first time, caused them to catch their breath in surprise at her beauty and sweetness. But I almost didn't take her home from the shelter when I first met her. I thought I needed to rescue a cat more…well, one more difficult to adopt than this gorgeous, fluffy, long-haired, part-Persian, adoring, green-eyed creature. I fell instantly in love with her. She had impossibly soft fur, she was gentle and sweet, and I was simply mesmerized by her. She would greet me at the door when I would come into the shelter kitty room, and I could practically hear her shouting at me: "*Hey!* I'm the one! I'm going home with you!" I had been going to the shelter to find a cat for several days, hoping to just know when I had found the right cat. Though I'd loved many of them, I just hadn't felt sure. After seeing June for two days in a row, I decided to give it one more day and see if someone put in an adoption application for her. That would be my sign: if no one put in an application for her, I would know she was the one! Sure enough, someone put in an application for her within one day. I was heartbroken. I asked the women at the shelter if anyone had ever put in a second adoption request for a cat before. She said no, but why not do it anyway? I put a request and application in for her just in case the first person changed his or her mind. One week later, when the time came for June to be picked up from the shelter, at the very last minute, my phone rang. The other person no longer wanted June! I ran down to the shelter and took my girl home immediately. Upon arriving, she acted as though she had lived with me forever. We lived happily ever after for four and a half wonderful years together. I know that I was blessed by her so deeply and that, in the end, maybe it was she who rescued me.

~ *Sandra Zeldes*

Sandra Zeldes *is a chef, healer, animal lover, singer/songwriter, proud auntie, and lover of antiques and rare things. You can find her at EatLikeAGoddess.com.*

Puffy

Sitting on the deck of my new home, I saw a cat walking on the fence. I thought, "Awww, isn't she cute?" and called, "Come here, kitty." She ran to me, jumped on my chair, and meowed repeatedly. I touched her, and she rolled on her back and meowed for me to pet her tummy. When I did, she purred louder. Her ability to trust so quickly was inspiring. After a few minutes I said, "Time for you to go home." I left her and thought nothing of it. The next morning I woke up and opened the drapes, and there she was! The more I resisted her affections, the more she persisted. A week later it was obvious she was on her own, so I fed her, but she wouldn't eat. Repeatedly she looked at me and looked at the food. "Oh no," I thought. I reluctantly said, "I love you," and she ate immediately. That is when I knew this kitten was a gift specifically meant for me. My cat, Magmurs, who had died only two weeks earlier, wouldn't eat until I said I love you. That is when Puffy got a name and became family.

~ Carol Lynn Fletcher

Carol Lynn Fletcher *is a writer, intuitive, graphic designer, and virtual assistant in the San Francisco Bay Area. You can reach her at FletcherBiz.com.*

Self-Trained Service Dog

My dog and I both feel a deep gratitude for each other—she because I rescued her from a difficult life with an uncertain future as a stray, and I because she has taught me that dogs can have special qualities. I've had dogs before, but I'm a "cat person" and always regarded dogs as mostly eating and barking machines. Babe, despite having lost a leg due to cruelty, has shown through her remarkable intelligence that she could have been a service dog. She takes care of me. After another dog knocked me down (and out) last year, she now waits with me at the top of the stairs until the coast is clear, then descends the steps with me in case I need help balancing. She alerts me to visitors before I hear them, and calls to me when the cats are having a dispute. She shakes her head to jingle her tags when she wants to go out because I might not know one bark from another. She walks with me without a leash, and always waits to be invited back into the house. I didn't have to train her. She's been training me!

~ *RJ Peters*

Dr. RJ Peters, *a retired physician, established a rescue shelter in 2002. She can be reached at Twitter.com/DrBert, and her dog is at ADogWith3Legs.blogspot.com.*

The Secret to Love Has Fur

Dreams do come true, even ones you might have forgotten. All it takes is love—and 22 years. Cosmo was a laid-back giant of a Cane Corso who loved to go to the dog park. There, in the spring of 2004, my destiny was dished up like a bowl of kibble. While Cosmo romped through the wet grass with his canine buddies, we pet-parents chuckled at each others' tales of triumph and woe regarding housebreaking and various other dastardly high jinks. Driving home, I couldn't stop smiling while reflecting on the joy we had experienced from sharing our stories about our beloved pets. I began to contemplate how everyone could tell their own unique and personal story. Simple: I'd create a magazine!

As the publisher of *Petpalooza,* a free print and online pet magazine, my first act was naming Cosmo to be C.E.D. (Chief Executive Dog). He was a natural. "Cosmo's Corner" led off each issue with a canine sound bite of fur-flavored wisdom. He was the face and heart of *Petpalooza.* Then devastation came: in May 2008, I lost Cosmo to osteosarcoma (in layman's terms: bone cancer, in my heartbroken terms: f*****g cancer). I didn't just lose my dog; I lost my roommate (I was a bachelor, never married), I lost my business partner, I lost my best friend, and I almost lost my way—but again love intervened.

Initially, I had contemplated ending *Petpalooza.* Without Cosmo, the magazine seemed pointless. As word spread of Cosmo's passing, an outpouring of love and support from *Petpalooza's* loyal readers and faithful advertisers buoyed my spirit. I began to believe that Cosmo could live on through the pages of *Petpalooza*. Fast-forward to that dream I might have forgotten: in 2009, I received a call from a woman who said she loved *Petpalooza*. She said she'd been reading it for years and would love to write an article. "Oh, and by the way," she added, "You may not remember, but back in the 80s you dated my sister, Lenore, in high school. Remember?" Yes, I remembered. I had loved her. Funny how love goes 'round. It had flowered in a park, with the help of my four-legged friend, to whom I will be eternally grateful. Dreams do come true. Lenore and I married in 2009.

~ Clyde LeFevre

Clyde LeFevre *is the publisher of* Petpalooza *magazine and founder of Petwoo.com. For more on "The Secret to Love has Fur," visit Petpalooza.com.*

My Beloved First Kitten

One day when I was 12, I was sitting on the porch, and a wild cat and her two kittens came up. They were afraid of humans. To avoid scaring them, I put food out and sat very quietly watching them eat, attempting to earn their trust. I tried to pet them periodically, and one day, to my delight, the male kitten jumped on my lap for the first time and let me pet him. I was getting cold, as it was fall, and I wanted to put him down so I could go inside, but I was afraid that would scare him. When I finally picked him up and put him on the stair, he wasn't scared. My parents didn't like cats, but because I spent many hours sitting on the porch taming the male kitten, they let me keep him because I earned it. That was one of the most joyous days of my life; I gained the trust of a wild kitten who became my pet and trusted friend. I'm middle-aged now and love and enjoy my two 10-year-old cats.

~ Avery Thurman

Avery Thurman *is a nurse with entrepreneurial goals. She loves being with her friends, spending time with her pets, and traveling. Find her at Facebook.com/AveryThurman.*

Star Brings Joy

One day my partner, Renee, announced that one of her students offered her a gift: a new puppy. I was reluctant. "A puppy?" I could only imagine the chaos. "I have always wanted a Yorkie," Renn explained. How could I refuse? When Star arrived, it was obvious that this dog was not a Yorkie. "Are you sure you want her?" I asked. Renee replied with a finality that was clear: "Her mother was a Yorkie, and this dog needs a home." That was that.

Star seemed to have two settings: "off" and "high." We bonded immediately. She was energetic, though earnest, and a quick learner. Our time together was cut short when tragic news arrived with a force that shook our family: Renee, my longtime soulmate, was diagnosed with advanced terminal cancer. Everything changed. As Renee's primary caregiver, I found Star, the puppy, too energetic for our circumstances. Letting go of Star carried with it a great sadness; perhaps she represented all the letting go. I was heartbroken. Four months passed. With Renee's death only days away, happiness was a distant memory. The house was so quiet. Then, out of the blue, I received a phone call: "We found your dog," the person on the phone announced. "What dog?" It was Star! She was found 40 miles away and still had her older tags, so I was called. When we reunited, Star leaped into my arms and fell asleep—as if to say "I am home!" Star could have just as easily been named "Joy" for what she gave me in the months that followed Renee's death. Star learned to catch a frisbee, and we played every day. She became a shining light in a difficult time. Today, Star remains my joyful companion, frisbee dog, and friend.

~ *Denise Rushing*

Denise Rushing *is permaculture educator in Upper Lake, Calif. She specializes in the transformation of individual and human systems. Learn more about Denise at DeniseRushing.com.*

Therapy Seizure Cats

Diagnosed with an inoperable brain tumor in 2002, I wanted something to help me feel better. I decided to get a kitten as a companion and brought 6-week-old BooBoo Kitty home. Six months later BooBoo's mother had another litter, and I brought home MewMew Kitty. They are my angels. They talk all the time, and I love it when they line up their toys or place them in a perfect circle on the floor. Most importantly, for the last eight years they have been therapy cats for me. After saving my life several times, they were certified by my neurologist as therapy seizure cats! When I have a seizure they wake me up by biting my nose, licking me, and even putting their paws in my mouth. They are always on the alert for my health. In May 2009 my apartment building burned in a four-alarm fire. I actually suffered a stroke because I believed they perished in the fire. When firefighters went back the next morning to search again, they found BooBoo and MewMew hidden under the bed, alive and well.

~ Glen Schallman

Glen Schallman, *born with an inoperable brain tumor, is a 52-year-old survivor, miracle, and hero! Friend him on Facebook to see pictures of his cats.*

Woofy

Dear Woofy

Dear Woofy,

On all the days that I am not able to give my mommy a loving hug, a squeeze, and a kiss, you are always there. I am so grateful for your furry loving kindness. Mommy doesn't remember much of anything at 90 years old. Well into dementia, she is a quiet, silver-haired Buddha. No one can say what you two talk about. You're by her side, always attentive, glancing up with your compassionate eyes, sitting in her lap, and receiving the love pats and sweet whispers that she showers into your ear. You two are always engaged in some kind of secret dialogue. Best of all, when you jump up suddenly from her lap, barking and running frantically after shadows on the wall and passing voices from the outside world, she laughs with abandon and squeals like a 5-year-old girl, forever young. Thank you, Woofy—small of stature and giant of heart.

Big Squeeze and Hug,
Ann

~ Ann Bennett

Ann Bennett *is a marketing coach known as "the creative genius" who helps entrepreneurs to attract more clients. You can contact her at Ann@IrresistibleMarketing.net.*

Puppy Love

There is something magical about seeing a Golden or Labrador Retriever puppy that makes your heart melt and your brain useless. You *will* buy one, so buyer beware! We bought our second Golden puppy for our two young children as a holiday surprise. My husband made an excuse on Christmas morning to run out and get some milk, and he came home with a box with a big red bow on top. I will never forget the wonder of them excitedly opening that box and seeing that adorable ball of fur wiggling out to survey his new surroundings. Thus began our 14-year love affair with MacGyver, who grabbed our heartstrings from day one and never let go. Our current princess is a Yellow Lab named Maggie May, who is 1½ years old. As empty-nesters, we struggled with getting another dog versus enjoying our footloose freedom. We decided that life without a dog was just not quite complete, and we could not be happier with our decision. She brings so much joy, love, and innocence into our lives—and watching her run to catch a ball in the sparkling ocean surf is simply the best.

~ Mary Armstrong Hines

Mary Armstrong Hines *is a teacher and social worker in the San Francisco Bay Area and can be reached at MaryH11@att.net.*

My Dream Cat, Finally

I lost count of the number of cats I'd looked at in response to our missing cat ad, and I hoped that evening's appointment wouldn't end in another heartbreak. The woman said she'd put the stray in a bedroom to keep him away from her two dogs. She opened the door, and the cat started down the hall. I stared, astonished. About 15 years earlier, I'd fallen in love with the picture of an orange and white tabby on the dust cover of a book, instantly deciding that if I would ever have a cat, I wanted one just like that one. Now, there he was, coming toward me. I could hardly believe it. He stopped at my feet, looked up, and then jumped into my lap. He snuggled down, curled into a ball, and purred contentedly as I began to pet his head. In spite of wandering around the trailer park for more than six weeks, he appeared healthy. I asked the woman a few questions and, satisfied with her answers, a few minutes later the newly named Cuddles and I left for his new home—at my house.

~ *Joyce Heiser*

Joyce Heiser *is a freelance author. She is widely published, mostly in the inspirational area. You can reach her at JoyceHeiser.com.*

I Enjoy Contemplating This

Rare treasures can occasionally be found in dumping grounds. So it was with Char. Hidden among the typical finds at the animal shelter was a pedigree Basenji. Curious about this breed, we read about it. The Basenji was supposedly employed by Egyptian pharaohs and their households during hunting expeditions. The Basenji's unique characteristic—it doesn't bark—made it the ideal dog for locating animals without revealing the pharaoh and his fellow hunters to the prey. True to form, Char didn't bark. However, unlike her ancestors, she wasn't employed in hunting escapades. Instead, friendly, affectionate Char became a beloved member of an American Jewish household.

Rare treasures can also be found among biblical verses. For example, consider Exodus 11:7: "And against the Children of Israel no dog shall whet its tongue." At the time when the Hebrew slaves were about to leave Egypt, God informed them that no dog would bark, thereby concealing their imminent escape. Could it be that the dogs alluded to in this particular verse were Basenjis? Is it possible that ancestors of Char were present when our family's ancestors were liberated from ancient Egypt? I enjoy contemplating this.

~ *Tziporah Wishky*

Tziporah Wishky, *from New Jersey, lives in Israel. She is a Torah teacher and life coach to women worldwide. Learn more at IStillHaveMyLife.com.*

Unassumingly, Tumblina

About 10 years ago, a petite female kitten quite literally tumbled into my life and catapulted her way into my heart. Tumbles, as she was first named, was found in a park and rescued from ill-intentioned teens. Like her brother, Bee Bop, found three weeks earlier, Tumbles was diagnosed with cerebellar hypoplasia, a challenging disorder that causes tremors and uncoordinated movements. To my amazement, Tumbles managed her disability remarkably well. Occasionally, she would catapult herself into my arms, but it was always a welcome surprise! When she catapulted, she flew through the air as if she had wings. She was truly light on her feet, like a little ballerina.

As the years passed, Tumbles became affectionately known as Tumblina. Despite her awkwardness, she maintained her sophistication and daintiness. I nicknamed her Garbo. She was patient with herself and others, especially her brother. She tolerated his complaints and suffered through his landings and inappropriate bed arrangements. She was patient with me. She followed me, gently requesting to be fed. She would look up at me and softly meow from her bed to say hello or make me stop working and kiss her. She mothered kittens, ferrets, and her other adult housemates. They learned to play with her at her capacity. She cuddled with her boyfriends and shared sunlit spaces with her girlfriend.

Tumblina developed seizures when she was 5 years old. She didn't let this stop her either; she was going to live her life! My little girl enjoyed another three years of catnip, belly rubs, feather toys, and the attention of men. She silently dealt with her illness, probably days before I knew she was sick. She looked at me one day as if to say "I just can't eat, but I'll try for you." That was a Wednesday night. On Thursday we went to the hospital. She enjoyed that car ride over the bridge. She commented often. Her eyes were bright, her tongue was sticking out slightly, as it often did, and she was smiling. When I arrived home from work Friday night, she called to me from her bed and passed in my arms. Tumblina passed the way she lived her life: unassumingly. She relished life and its small wonders. Her eyes were always bright and wide with curiosity. She taught me appreciation, humility, perseverance, and tolerance. I am truly blessed to have known such a wonderful, generous soul.

~ Kerry A. See

Kerry A. See *is a pet-care business owner, Reiki practitioner, animal rescuer, pet product designer, baker, gardener, and aspiring writer. Contact her at RufflyPurrfect.com.*

Jazzy: Conjurer of Miracles

After bringing me up-to-date on Jazzy's condition, the doctor paused for a brief moment of reflection, then looked at me and quietly said, "She's a miracle." Tears welled in my eyes at the simplicity and wisdom of her words. I sobbed, giving thanks that my beautiful angel-in-kitty-clothes was still with me. It was early October 2009, and Jazzy had been valiantly fighting for her life for 96 hours. Before I tell you how she's doing today, you need to know that the first miracle Jazzy performed was surviving an encounter with a car when she was quite young. Following a brief stay with a nearby veterinarian, she was miraculously adopted by some neighbors who are unabashed animal lovers. She lived with them for five years, and then we met. "Love at first sight" is how Jazzy's previous companions described it.

Because of the bond Jazzy and I shared, her companions gave her to me when they moved: miracle number three. Several years later, Jazzy and I were separated. Other than an occasional short visit, we were apart for nearly three years. Miracle number four: despite a severe bout of pancreatitis, she survived, and we were finally on schedule to be reunited. But just days prior to our coming together again, Jazzy fell ill—terribly ill. Not only was she suffering from ketoacidosis and elevated liver enzymes, frighteningly, her red blood cell count had fallen to 12%, which, as one doctor phrased it, is not life-supporting. Several intense days and three transfusions later, she began to recover: major miracle number five.

Today, 18 months and a move across country later, I am elated to tell you she has fully recovered. I now have the distinct honor of living with her on a daily basis and watching as she continues to thrive. Miracle six: she is 16 years old. Of course I have no idea how much more time I have with her, but whatever amount it may be, it will not be enough—it could never be enough. I often tell her, "Sweet Pea, if I had a million years with you, when those were through, I'd ask for a billion more." I am immensely and eternally grateful for the presence and love of my wise, steadfast, and miraculous friend, Jazzy.

~ Ken Collier

Ken Collier *is honored to have known Jazzy 11 years so far. He works with grieving people who have lost a beloved animal companion. He can be reached via e-mail at Ken@DiscoveryJourneys.net.*

Is it Negotiable?

Years ago my daughter and I were looking to rent a second home. We had moved to a new city a year before with only two bags and a teddy bear. During that time we often felt alone—after all, we didn't know many people, and everything was different, even the stars in the sky. One day we spotted some puppies for sale. It was love at first sight with one white puppy making an extra effort to get our attention! Apple became part of our family. She was there to make us laugh every day and help us through the rough times. She followed us and stood by our sides many times, filled a void, and helped us grow. That day when we were looking for a new home, we asked if they allowed pets and were told no. The woman asked, "Is it negotiable? Could you give the dog away?" Negotiable?! Would you trade someone who stays by your side at all times—no questions asked, no judgments made—in exchange for some empty walls? In unison, we gladly said, "*No!*" That home was not meant to be ours, as giving away Apple was certainly *not* negotiable.

~ Shahar Boyayan

Shahar Boyayan *is an innovative marketing advisor for entre-preneurs, and is crazy for animals and geocaching.*

Our Angel-on-Loan

We knew he wasn't ours to keep. All wiggles and snuffles, 7-week-old Jordy was our third puppy to raise for Seeing Eye. He stole our hearts instantly, and it would be devastating to say good-bye 16 months later when our job of raising him was done. He was adorable—what Labrador puppy isn't? A uniquely dark caramel, he had an "old man" wrinkled face. Those deep brown eyes conveyed a loving disposition and sincere desire to please, and his tail never stopped wagging. Jordy seemed uncommonly bright. He was easy to house-train, and who could be too upset by an occasional "oops" when he looked so ashamed and repentant? He was a quick study; he learned the basic commands rapidly, and became a model canine good citizen. Clearly special, he exhibited a depth of soul and connection to "his" humans beyond anything we had experienced before. I called him our "angel dog," for the knowing way about him and his amazing anticipation of everyone's thoughts and moods. These traits would make him even more able to guide and protect a blind person.

My fondest memory of Jordy was as my laundry assistant. One time he was beside me on the porch as I hung the wash. I dropped a sock, absently saying "Uh-oh!" On cue, Jordy trotted down the steps, gently retrieved the sock, and proudly delivered it to me. From then on, he stood guard over my actions as laundry master, dutifully and joyfully retrieving every sock I "accidentally" dropped, saying, "Uh-oh, Jordy. Get it!" He must have thought I was hopelessly clumsy!

The dreaded day came to return him to Seeing Eye for

advanced training to prepare him for his destiny. We cried to see him go, but it was the bargain we had to keep. He passed his training with ease, and we saw him once more, from a distance, walking the streets of Morristown in harness, with his trainer. Tears streamed from under my sunglasses—tears of sadness and of pride. He went home with his new owner in a closed adoption; we never met her or knew her name. Yet, when I read the letter telling of his final destiny, I wept with joy to know that our "angel dog" went to a 17-year-old high school senior, and that he would take her off to college that fall. I believe it was a match made in Heaven.

~ *Gail Patterson*

Gail Patterson *is the Women's Envisionary, helping midlife women meet the changes and challenges they face today. Get to know her at WiseWomansWay.com.*

Three Blessed Pets

I can only think that somehow, there is a match-up guru in heaven for pets and owners. I have never knowingly shopped for a pet, yet have been blessed with three. While new-car shopping, the smallest of kittens dropped down from beneath a Toyota Celica, with a meow so loud my husband could only describe it as a "geshrai," Yiddish slang for a blood-curdling scream! So began our 20-year love affair with Celica, our feisty feline who thought he was a dog.

Claiming he was not pet shopping, my husband absent-mindedly visited St. Hubert's Animal Welfare Center and was immediately drawn to the dog who ignored him. We had to have her, my husband said, because Sadie was named after his mother—and she looked at him with that same disdain in her eyes. Rechristened Sasha, our Husky/Collie rescue became the love of our entire family for 10 great years.

Dreaming of a black-and-white dog encouraged my husband to look to Mount Pleasant Kennels, guaranteed to be the place we "must go" by our niece. Awaiting us, of course, was our Border Collie/Collie rescue, twice returned and slated for goose patrol. Today, we love the excitement of agility with Bela, our black-and-white, beautiful, not-so-incorrigible boy!

~ *Cecelia Heckman Inwentarz*

Cecelia Heckman Inwentarz, *author of* Become The Butterfly—Experience Heartfelt Energy, *is a practitioner of therapeutic energy medicine and energy psychology. Learn more at TheCHiEnergist.com.*

All Pets Go to Heaven

Pets that are small or big and live in water, on land, in your living room, or in your bedroom all have one thing in common: they all go to heaven. Their job on earth is simple and profound. You see, the beauty of their job is to just be who they are. Think about that—just to be who they are. If only we could adopt their job as humans. Pets are powerful teachers for demonstrating how to love and be loved unconditionally. Eyes that melt you like sun on ice cream communicate in the language of one soul to another. We listen more attentively when words vanish and emotion speaks. We hug more when we are not judged. We share more sincerely when we are just listened to.

When our pets depart, our hearts break. I hear owners say, "I miss him, and I need to know he is okay" and "She was my best friend." Just as quickly as they share their grief to me, I hear their beloved pets sending me all kinds of messages about love, thankful and wanting to help. Love is a powerful force that never dies; it only transforms. Always know they are still listening, and they still love you.

~ *Louise Rouse*

Louise Rouse *is a coach with the amazing gift of being able to help you connect with your pets in Heaven.*
Visit InvisibleRelationships.com for more information.

Who Rescued Who?

My husband and I never had kids. Instead we "rescue" animals and give them our love. It is they, our FurKids, who have taught us the most valuable things in life:

Families are made of much more than humans.

Love and tears, hope and laughter, precious memory-making, the value of an unquenchable spirit.

Being happy about the simple things in life.

Food, walks, nose nudges.

Playing all full-out, soaking up sun, laying in the grass.

The value of curiosity:

Slowing down enough to come nose-to-nose with a deer.

Watching an insect crawl.

Confidence: never give up on what you want.

Encouragement: the quiet touch of a paw.

The signal that "all is well" from a purr, a lick, a look, or just being a present calming presence by our side.

Celebration and comfort... compassion.

Pain may be inevitable, but suffering is optional...faith, persistence, and peace prevail.

FurKids never judge themselves. When they see themselves in the mirror, they're just curious...

Movement with grace and pride

And in the darkest times... we learned family is where our hearts feel most at home, always wanted, always welcomed, always needed, always loved.

So who really rescued who?

~Teresa C. Lea

Teresa C. Lea *shows people how to heal, reclaim their lives, and step into authenticity and personal power. You can reach her at InTouchInLife.com.*

CPSIA information can be obtained at www.ICGtesting.com
Printed in the USA
BVOW021033150911

271109BV00004B/4/P